SMASHING SELF-EMPLOYMENT

THE ULTIMATE GUIDE TO SELF-EMPLOYMENT SURVIVAL AND SUCCESS

By Karl Craig-West
www.smashingselfemployment.com

COPYRIGHT

Karl Craig-West has asserted his right as the author of this work and the owner of the copyright in accordance with the Copyrights, Design and Patents Act 1988.

No part of this publication may be resold, hired out, lent, or reproduced in any form or by any means without the express consent of the the author and/or his agents.

First published in the United Kingdom in 2017
Copyright © 2017 Karl Craig-West
Design by Clare McCabe, www.purplestardesign.co.uk

www.smashingselfemployment.com

All rights reserved.
ISBN-13: 978-1979303842

DISCLAIMER

The contents of this book do not constitute advice and is not intended as a substitute for professional business advice.
This book is published in good faith but neither the publisher or the author shall be held liable for any alleged damage arising from any suggestion or information contained in this book.

THANKS TO:

Erica Brown *who convinced me to make a start.*

Paul Chapman and Jodie Bidder *who both stayed on my case about 'getting it done'.*

Janet Shaughnessy *for her superb transcribing skills.*

Clare McCabe (my designer) *for her patience.*

God *for always being there.*

And last, but by no means least, my wonderful better-half Emma *who loves me despite of it all, isn't afraid to tell me I'm wrong and (at least outwardly) doesn't laugh at my ideas.*

Thanks to you all - this book wouldn't have happened without any of you

FOREWORD
by Paul Chapman
Author, Speaker and co-founder of Marketing Jumpleads

So here's the problem...

We are not supposed to be self-employed.

Almost everything in our education sets us up for a job, a salary and the ability to get paid for what we are good at - whatever that is.

But there is one teeny, tiny, glaring error in the whole plan – a lot of us are actually self-employed. Some through choice, some through necessity.

This has been compounded over the last few years where we have seen a bruised economy thrust more people out on their own. Whilst many are well equipped to do the "function" of their business, most are ill-equipped at all to actually RUN a business. And that is a big problem.

The business world is riddled with businesses that were good at what they actually did, but failed because they couldn't properly manage themselves and their business.   Often the two things go hand in hand.

That's why this book is so important. Whilst there are a myriad of books out there, very few (if any) actually talk about the simple day to day realities and addresses the challenges that self-employed people often have. From the outside world these issues can seem almost "too small" but as a self employed person - especially one coming from the world of employment - they are critical and can save a whole host of frustration, pain, and cost further down the line. Experience shows that self-employed business owners do need real help with all the peripheral stuff (annoyingly, the stuff that makes the difference). You can be the best at what you do but your business will fail if you can't manage yourself as a business.

Things like how to set your prices, networking, getting your first customer and even how to deal with the awkward ones (you'll get a few of those!) have nothing to do with how good you are at something. But they have everything to do with getting your business into year two and beyond.

Thankfully though – in the shape of this book - help is at hand. Real, practical advice about the REAL things you need to think about when you are thinking about self-employment.

And most importantly it comes from a real business owner. Someone who has built his own business from scratch and continues to run it successfully today. And that is really important. There are a LOT of self styled business gurus out there and, worryingly, a lot of them have never run their own business and don't do now.

That isn't to say these people can't be really useful to you, but unless you're running a small business it's hard to know what the day to day stresses of self-employment and business ownership, particularly when small and starting up, are like.

Real advice, on real issues from a real business owner is vital for any business success… and sanity. And that's why this book is a great place to start.

Paul Chapman
www.marketingjumpleads.com

Smashing Self-Employment

Contents

Introduction 10

Getting Started

Chapter 1: It's Important To Know Why You're Doing What You Do 12

Chapter 2: Why You Need Some Kind Of Business Plan 16

Chapter 3: Setting Your Prices 29

Chapter 4: Getting Those First Few Customers 42

Chapter 5: What To Do On Your First Day 52

Chapter 6: Looking After The Money - Financial Planning And Managing Money 57

Up and Running

Chapter 7: Being Organised And Coping With Overwhelming Workloads 65

Chapter 8: Do What You Say And Build A Reputation 75

Chapter 9: Getting Your Marketing Right 79

Chapter 10: How To Make Sales Work For You 91

Chapter 11: Why You Should Hang Around With (and Learn From) The Right People 104

Chapter 12: Winning Momentum And Celebrating Success 110

Chapter 13: Why Goal Setting Is A Powerful Tool To Help You Make Your Dreams A Reality 117

Chapter 14: How To Deal With Awkward Customers 119

Chapter 15: Networking - How To Make It Work For You 128

Chapter 16: Why It Takes More Than Just Passion To Be Successful 136

Chapter 17: How To Coach Yourself Out Of Mental Blocks 138

Chapter 18: How To Deal With Staffers 141

Long-Term Success

Chapter 19: How Getting Proper Rest Can Actually Help You And Your Business 145

Chapter 20: Why Increasing Your Fees Is A Good Idea 148

Chapter 21: What To Do When Things Get Tough 153

Chapter 22: Realising That "You Are It" 160

Chapter 23: Improving Your Business With CRM And Automation 166

Chapter 24: Moving From Self-Employed To Business Owner 175

Introduction

Hi, and thanks for buying this book.

If you're anything like a typical self-employed person you'll know the challenges that come with being your own boss and also being a one-person-business. Things like the stress of having not enough money, not enough hours in the day, dealing with awkward customers (who often don't pay anywhere near on time), and having to juggle so many different roles and loads more besides.

But I have some good news (and some not-so good news).

The good news is that, within this book, you'll learn some simple and down-to-earth ways for making your life easier. This includes things like: getting more done, winning more customers, keeping customers happy (and making sure you get paid), reducing stress, having more control and maybe even having a day off without feeling guilty.

Overall you'll learn how to fight and often win the many battles that come your way when running yourself as a small business.

The not-so-good news is that you're going to have to put in some effort if you're truly going to start moving forward. Just knowing this stuff won't help, you'll actually have to do something with the knowledge for it to serve.

I'm not going to pull any punches. Being self-employed can be tough and you're going to have to be tough at times if you're going to survive and thrive. That means being honest with yourself and confronting reality (and all that it entails).

Having said that, there is plenty of good stuff and, throughout the book, the constant aim is to help you make your life and your business much more successful.

Introduction

Now, you might be wondering just how I know all of this stuff. Well, for most of my adult life I've been self-employed and met a wide range of success and failure. Even to the point where I went bankrupt in 2008.

However, this is no rags-to-riches story; getting rich isn't really my aim. However, I know that financial success and security is an important motive for many self-employed people. The point of this book is to share the things I've learned that I now apply to my life and business to make it the success that it is with the aim of helping you to a greater level of success too, whether that's in financial terms, independence, time or just being able to do things in the way you like to do them.

The chapters are largely self-contained which means that you can read it in small chunks Which is great if you don't feel that you have the time to sit and read it all in one session.

So, dig into the book and enjoy the lessons.

All the best regards,

Karl Craig-West

p.s. You can find loads of resources, based on the material in this book at: www.smashingselfemplyment.com/book-resources

Chapter 1
It's Important To Know Why You're Doing What You Do

There's much to learn to be successful at self-employment but (arguably) the first thing to really take on board is that YOU NEED TO KNOW WHY YOU'RE DOING IT.

People become self-employed for a wide variety of reasons. For some it's a natural part of building a career. For others it's a case of 'can't find a job so I'll give this a go'. Some, like me, have always wanted to have my own business. And then there's the army of people who get made redundant and decide to start selling what they used to do for someone else in order to make a living.

Your route to self-employment doesn't really matter. What matters here is why you're doing it.

And this 'why' needs to be big, bright and very clear in your mind.

So, have you ever stopped and asked yourself why you're doing this? I mean, really stopped and thought about it.

The reason I'm asking so emphatically is because if you're unclear as to what your motivation is (and motivation is simply a reason for doing something) then when it gets tough you'll question yourself.

"Your WHY needs to be big, bright and very clear in your mind!"

Getting Started

And I don't just mean you'll question why you're doing it. You'll also question your own abilities, your decision-making, and (worst of all) you'll question whether you've made a big mistake and whether you're really cut out for this.

And this can become very soul-destroying and very damaging for your self-esteem along with it.

OK, enough of all this doom and gloom stuff. Let's get to the point.

The point is this: **without a very clear WHY you'll struggle**.

When things get tough, and they absolutely definitely will at some point, it's this 'why' that will keep you going.

It'll help to get you out of bed in the mornings. It'll spur you on when you're working through the ten o'clock news to get something done that's needed the following morning. It'll help you when you're up at silly-o'clock to get to your breakfast networking meeting. It'll help you when your worst client has just had another whinge at you about something he feels you've done wrong.

So, here's a few examples to get your motivational juices flowing:

- Do you want make a living and/or provide for your family?
- Do you want the flexibility of being to able to (for example) go to your child's sports day without having ask the boss or arrange someone to cover for you?
- Do you want to make a lot of money (or at least do better than you did while working for someone else)?
- Do you have an idea that you think will take the world by storm?
- Are you sick of working for someone else and just want the freedom to do 'your' thing?

Personally, I have a few motivations. I love being able to go to school events to watch my kids, I love the flexibility to choose what I'm working on, and I really don't enjoy working for anyone else.

Oh, and every now and then, the money is pretty good too.

So, here's what we want you to do right now. I promise it'll help you a lot.

1 -- Find some space in a **quiet-ish environment** where you're unlikely to be interrupted for half an hour or so. Switch off the phone, the computer, the radio, the television. The key is to give yourself some thinking room.

2 -- Next, get a **blank piece of paper and a pen**.

3 -- Now **start writing down the reason**, or reasons, why you're self-employed. Just write down whatever comes to mind, even if it's a little vague or very personal to you. Don't exclude anything at all, everything counts on this list.

Take your time, don't rush, there are no right or wrong answers here.

What you're doing in this exercise is reinforcing your motivation through the physical act of writing it down. And this will help these key motivators to stick more firmly in your mind.

Ideally you want to put this sheet in a place where you can see it regularly, preferably every day. Again, the idea here is to help make these

> "Your 'why' will help you to keep going when things get tough!"

Getting Started

thoughts stick in your mind so being able to see it and read it frequently will make them strong and immovable over time. Now I know that some folks will say: "Well I have my motivation clear in my mind, so why should I bother writing it down?"

The answer to that is very simple: Your conscious mind only has so much space at any one time. And when you get stressed with work or hassled by a client it's very easy for those all-encompassing thoughts to drown out your ability to keep your motivation in mind.

So, a daily reminder will mean that the things you're working for will always be strong, no matter what the world throws at you.

Just a quick assurance though: you don't have to show this sheet to anyone else. It's your motivation. If you choose to share it with your partner or someone close to you then that's fine but please bear in mind that they may not completely understand your rationale here, especially if they're a career employee.

What you'll quickly learn is that those who've only worked for someone else will never understand the challenges of those who are self-employed. But we'll come onto this later in the book.

One key thing to remember about this list is that it will never be static. Six months after starting out your motivations are likely to be different. So, go through the exercise on a periodic basis. As often as you feel is required really.

So, to summarise:
Make sure you know why you're doing it. When things get tough, this motivation will be your driving force. You need to have a crystal clear picture of **why** you're in it. Without it you'll struggle.

Chapter 2
Why You Need Some Kind of Business Plan

Whether you run a business with employees or you're a self-employed sole trader, you need a plan. A plan is simply identifying your main goals and how you're going to achieve those goals.

I know a lot of people who run small businesses and are self-employed. But probably as many as 80% of them don't have a proper plan for what they're doing in their business, about where they're going or what they're trying to achieve, never mind how they're going to make it all happen.

So in this chapter I'll be discussing the key things that you need to plan. If you have a good plan and actually follow it, the odds of you succeeding in the small business world will be much higher.

What is a plan?

So, what do we mean by plan? It's essentially the strategy you devise to reach your goals. We plan all the time - whether it's decorating the house or getting fit. And we know that there's a much higher chance of succeeding if we have a plan to do it. And it's particularly true for business. You identify what you want to achieve in the

> "Without some kind of plan your progress will be haphazard at best, non-existent at worst!"

Getting Started

long term and set out a step-by-step series of actions, or performance indicators, or micro goals. Each of these regular and consistent contributions will help you to meet those long term goals.

Your Business Plan

So where do you start? Well, think of a business plan like a set of directions for your business that set out **how** you want your business to run and **what** you hope to achieve. And, as I'll explain below, it can cover a range of issues and can be in any format that works for you.

The plan could be a list of points on the back of an envelope, or a formal document that has pages full of detailed information, from product specs to detailed budgeting, to skills required for key members of staff. Either way, you'll find that putting together all of those ideas that have been running round in your head is a really good motivator because you finally SEE how your ideas can meld to become a real businesses. It doesn't have to be perfect but you have to start somewhere.

Of course, the bigger and more complex the business, the more information you'd need to include in a business plan. If you want to borrow money from a bank or investors, you WILL need a formal and detailed plan to present to the bank manager or investor. These can take a long time to prepare, even if you're only asking to borrow a few thousands of pounds.

Your business plan means that you know what you'll be doing and give some structure to your activities. It's also essential to give yourself some "instructions" because, unless you're very disciplined, it's easy to go off on a tangent and get lose sight of the big picture. You might have the best possible product in the world but it's no good if you don't have the right premises or any customers.

And this is especially true if you've never run a business or been self-employed before. If you've spent most or all of your working life working for other people, you're used to turning up at 9am and doing whatever you're told until 5pm. When you work for yourself, you're both the boss and the employee, so you have to tell yourself what to do.

If you want your self-employment to be successful, then you have to be **committed** to making it work. It's like anything in life - decide what you want to achieve, work out a **plan** to do it and commit yourself to making it happen.

Write it down!

There are 2 very good reasons for writing it down. The physical act of writing it down will help you to remember the key points and, as you're writing, you'll see which parts of the plan need further work. Secondly, while your plan is a set of instructions, there will be times - probably a lot more than you anticipate - when you decide to change things. If you're not selling enough stuff, then you may need to change what you're selling OR you may need to put more effort into sales and marketing to get more customers in the door. You want to keep a record of what works and what doesn't as you go along.

What should it include?

At the very least, the plan needs to cover 5 main elements:

- Finance
- Budgeting
- Operation and development plan: big picture
- Work plan: the day to day stuff
- Sales and marketing

Getting Started

Financial Plan

Probably the first thing to consider is finance. Most of us work to earn a living, which means that you need to generate enough sales to generate a profit. And if you want your business to grow, you have to generate enough profits to fund the development and investment.

> "If you don't have a plan, then your work is likely to be chaotic and your capacity to earn is likely to be limited!"

Whether your main goal is to make a lot of money - perhaps with a new invention. developing a franchise or a new service line - or simply fund a certain level of lifestyle, you have to think about money.

But first, let's be a bit realistic about things.

Failing, surviving or succeeding.

We've all heard about people who become millionaires because they've come up with a dream product or some very clever service or franchising business. But they are the exception rather than the rule. You may also be aware of the statistic that around 90% of new businesses that fail in the first year do so because of financial reasons, even those whose owners spent a lot of time and effort on financial planning and were **ABSOLUTELY** certain that their business would make them a lot of money.

They typically fail because while their business idea may be fantastic, the owners haven't properly understood the true costs of being in business - for example the day to day issues of cash-flow, waiting for customers to pay or completely over-estimating the volume of sales because they haven't done the right sort of market research.

Find a good accountant

Finance is a complex subject. It's a lot more than just how much you sell and managing the cash-flow. There are several financial, tax and even some legal issues that you need to consider. If this is your first time in business, you'll be dealing with a lot of new things - for example whether you trade as an incorporated company, how much tax you'll have to pay, do you need to register for VAT (sales tax), whether to pay yourself a salary.......the list is endless. But it is really important to get this right.

> "Getting the financial side of things right means that you're much more likely to succeed!"

Getting the financial side of things right means that you're much more likely to be in the 10% of businesses that not only survive the first year, but preferably in the even smaller percentage that succeed, even if you don't become a millionaire.

So when it comes to finance, one of the best pieces of advice I can give is to **find a good accountant before you start trading**, someone you trust and who can help you to deal with the financial aspects of running a business. And take time and care finding the right person. **Don't sign up the first accountant you meet or the one with the cheapest price**. Your accountant will be an important part of your business team and will be trusted with a lot of personal and financial information about you and your business.

Ask other business owners for referrals and recommendations. Ask about their qualify of service. Compare their pricing and think about whether it's good value for money. Can you pay on a monthly basis? Is this someone you can work with on a long term basis? Do you like them personally? Do they have experience with your type of business?

Whatever size or type of business, whatever business sector you're in, you need to do your research and get on top of the financing issues as soon as you can. Understanding the financial side of things can make a huge difference to your bottom line. **Business owners who know how accounting, tax and other financial issues affect their businesses are always much more profitable because they're in control of their finances rather than having their finances control them.**

Budgeting

The other side to finance is the day to day aspect of budgeting. We all do it all the time - whether it's balancing our salary to pay the bills or having enough cash in our wallets or money in our accounts to buy new shoes for the kids.

If you become self-employed, the very first thing is to work out how you're going to survive until you start selling your goods or services. You need enough money both to fund the business costs - which could include product development costs, marketing costs, professional costs - and your own living expenses until you start earning enough income to pay yourself.

> "Getting the budgeting right from the start could make the difference between succeeding or failing!"

Budgeting is particularly important if you take out a bank loan or get funds from investors, because you have to demonstrate that the business is *financially viable down to the finest detail*. But even if you don't have to borrow any money, you still have to budget.

Suppose you work from home and your partner earns enough money to pay the mortgage and basic bills. This means that your income has to pay for your food and drink, cars, school fees, holidays AFTER your business costs. But how do you cope if your income isn't regular? What do you do if you have little or no income for a couple of months in a row, or you're just starting out and have no sales for the first few months?

Either way, getting the budgeting right from the start could make all the difference between succeeding or failing. Even if your costs are just a fraction more than your income most of the time, this mounts up over time. Businesses often fail simply because of rising deficits that build up because the owners haven't budgeted properly. Making just small changes to your expenditure could mean the difference between failing, surviving or succeeding.

Operational Plan

The operational plan is the practical side of your business - the logistics. How are you going to be working, getting the right premises, how you're going to deliver the goods or services, how you're going to organize your time or your employees or your subcontractors?

This is all about ***how*** your business will work - the big picture - because, if you don't have a plan, then your work is likely to be chaotic. Your capacity to earn is going to be limited by how much work you can get done and you'll probably end up being in constant panic mode.

This means organizing all of the important functions that make your self-employment function. For example, if you're selling goods online, then you need to organize a number of things:
- Buying or making products to sell.
- Finding customers - you'll need a website and an online presence so that people will visit your website and will

Getting Started

buy your products. It takes time to get a website and to develop an online customer base - I'll talk about this more in the chapter about marketing, but you have to get all of this set up before you can sell anything.
- What about payment methods and invoicing?
- How will you package the goods and how will you deliver them?
- What about the legal stuff; terms and conditions?

Your own business model may be less complicated, but regardless of the type of business, you need to understand how it will operate and make sure that you've covered all you need to get your business up and running.

A Work Plan

So now you can see the big picture, you need to work out how to do it on a day to day basis. Your work plan will help you do this. It doesn't have to be complicated; it could be as simple as how you're going to organize your week.

When you're an employee, you turn up at 9am and you do what you're told to do and when to do it. Now you have to manage your own activities. You need to develop a routine that allows you to work most efficiently, allocating time for customers, suppliers, marketing, the finances... you get the idea. Ideally, you'd have a personal assistant to run your diary, but most self-employed people don't have that luxury (at least to start with)! But your time is money so you need to use it carefully.

Early mornings

For example, I like getting important stuff done in the first part of every day, and that important stuff is usually my marketing. Why? Because that's the time when I'm at my sharpest, when I can more easily focus on details and deal with complex technical issues. So, I organize every single working day according to that. The first hour or so is always marketing. That's my key time to do my marketing and other productive "office" stuff.

I schedule meetings from lunchtime onwards because I don't want anything to dent my ability to get decent, productive work out of the way before lunch.

Tuesdays and time off

I try to use each day in most productively. For example, I try to keep Tuesdays free because, according to all the research, Tuesday is usually the most productive day of the week and I want that day to be set aside simply for doing client work. I also plan time in every single week to sit and think about the business and that's usually Fridays, late morning. I sit and think what we're doing, what have we achieved that week, what do we need to work on and plan for the following week, and other stuff like that.

You also need to make sure you have proper time off - family time, weekends, evenings, holidays to give you a chance to unwind and perform at your best. Do what works for you - if you have children, you might do the school runs and work in the evenings to keep up with things.

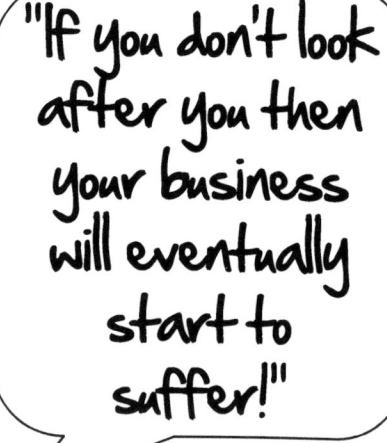

"If you don't look after you then your business will eventually start to suffer!"

Either way, remember that you're the most important resource in your business. Use your time efficiently and look after yourself. If you don't look after you then your business will eventually start to suffer.

Sales and Marketing

You can have the best product in the world, but it's not worth anything if you don't have any customers. That's why we also have a plan for our marketing and our target customers we want. We have sales targets, we have targets for leads and we have a plan for generating those leads.

Marketing is all about finding potential customers so that you can sell to them. It's all part of a single process.

<u>That's why I believe that the most important part of any business plan is the Sales and Marketing strategy.</u> And we'll be discussing this in much more detail in chapter 9.

But, even right from the start, you need to think about who you're selling to, what you're saying to them, and how you're getting that across, and then working out the best ways of marketing for your particular target market.

To begin with, you need to think about how you reach your target audience. How often are you going to reach your target audience, whether you use social media, email marketing, or postal marketing, or going to networking events, or advertising. You need to do your research and develop a plan for doing this.

> *"Getting & keeping customers (marketing) should be an essential part of every working day!"*

Marketing should be an everyday activity

We schedule a formal meeting each quarter to review our overall activity, which includes reviewing our marketing. If the "order book" is looking healthy and we have work lined up for the next 2 to 3 month, we know that our strategy is working. We also sit down once a month and share out the work so we know who's doing what and when.

But our marketing diary is an integral part of our work diary. We send out regular emails. We have daily social media. We write blog posts once a week. We write articles for other websites or publications once a week. We spend time writing up plans for additional products and services.

All of this has to be planned in and becomes part of our marketing process, because if we don't plan it then it's likely to never happen.

So, how can you do this? What do you want to get done this next quarter? What do you want to get done each month of that quarter? What activities do you need to do on a weekly basis within that month? And, then, what do you need to do every day?

For example, if you're a social media fan and looking for clients online, you should be doing social media pretty much every day. If you're into blogging and writing articles, you should be doing that once a week at the very least. If you're into sending emails out to your customers, like newsletters and useful stuff for your audience, you need to be doing that every two or three weeks.

Like any other activity, it forms part of your day to day schedule and it gets done because you've allocated time and it's in the planner. Planning is absolutely essential.

Stay calm and keep marketing....

Business is a fluid and flexible thing. You might have the most organised, structured business, but you'll always be reacting to the things you can't control. You respond to clients. You respond to demand. You respond to all sorts of other things that happen in your life, and in your business, and in your work. Even we all know that things don't always go to plan.

Getting Started

If you're having problems with customers, staff, cash-flow, the bank manager or even family issues, one of the first activities that often suffers is marketing. It can be difficult focusing on finding clients for next month or the month after when you're struggling to pay this month's rent and chasing existing clients for late payments.

But, that's why marketing is so important! You MUST plan your marketing and stick to the plan as much as possible because if you don't, chances are that your financial problems will be even worse next month because you'll have no new work lined up. If you don't plan your marketing and do it on a regular basis, chances are you'll never do it. Because, as and when you get busy, you'll be blown around responding to problems that come up every day. Even 20 to 30 minutes a day of routine marketing activity can make a significant difference for your business.

Plan Tomorrow Today

So, now you understand why you need a plan for your business. But you also have to put the plan into action and think about it on a regular basis. I think about our plan almost every single working day, even if it's only a few minutes, just to make sure that we're okay and heading in the right direction.

> "The day's not over until the next day's planned!"

And one of the most important things I do at the end of each working day is to plan the following day's activities.

Several years ago, I heard a business speaker say: "The day is not over until the next day is planned." You should never get into the office, ever sit down and think, "What am I doing today?" You always want to get the day rolling as soon as you start work, when you're at your most efficient. Always plan your following day -- always, always, always.

Final Points

So, I hope I've given you enough there on planning. I hope that there's plenty of things for you to take away from that. Whatever you do, plan your business before you start trading so that you have a well defined sense of direction.

Remember, planning is an on-going part of running a business, whether it's planning new product lines, finding larger premises, finding new investors.

In my opinion, the marketing plan is the most important part of your business plan because it's all about how you're going to bring in the customers and get paid. You might be able to function without an operational plan (if you don't mind things being a bit disorganised), but in my view you can't survive without a marketing plan.

I'd also strongly recommend that you have a work plan. It doesn't have to be written in stone, but schedule your day to day activities so that you make the most out of your limited time and schedule key times to do the key tasks.

Most of all, take time to review and plan your business as you go along.

Spend time planning and reviewing on a regular basis to see if your plans are working, even if you're working on your own. It's your business, so take time out away from the office, away from the work, switch the phone off, leave the computer alone, sit down, make some notes about how the business is performing.

Make sure that you're always planning ahead so that you know where your business is going.

Chapter 3
Setting Your Prices

In this chapter, I'm going to cover a grossly misunderstood and misinterpreted area of running a small business and being self-employed, and that is setting your prices.

In my experience, many people who start a small business grossly undervalue their work and what they're doing for their clients. And, as a result, they grossly under-price what they sell, which usually means that they'll be working long hours and not making much money.

And I can attest to this because, when I started our website design business, we were selling websites which I thought were competitively priced. But taking into account the amount of time that I spent on each website project versus how much I charged, I would have been financially better off working in a supermarket stacking shelves.

"Most businesses start out by underpricing what they sell!"

But, I have some good news: there's a few things that you can do to make sure that you don't work silly hours for no money because your pricing is completely wrong. You probably won't get your pricing right first time, and the chances are good you'll never get your pricing exactly right. But you certainly don't want to charge too little.

So, where do you start?

Let's start with some simple principles. Setting your prices always revolves around how much money you want to earn and then how much you can deliver with the number of hours you have.

So, let's look at a quick example. Now, imagine you've got a monthly income target of £2,000. That's not a huge amount of money in today's terms, but it's a good place to start. There are approximately, in a month, 20 working days. So, £2,000 divided by 20 gives you £100 a day. That's how much you need to earn to make £2,000 a month.

The first question you have to ask is whether that's £2,000 in profit (what you can take home) or is that simply £2,000 in turnover? Because, if it's turnover, then you need to think, "Well, how much am I going to make out of that after all of my business expenses are taken out of that?"

If you're offering a service, the margins - i.e. what you add to your cost to reach your selling price - are usually quite high. If you're offering a tangible product, maybe clothes, jewellery or IT equipment, then the margins are often a lot lower.

For example, if you want £2,000 worth of profit and you're selling jewellery and your margin is 20%, then you need to sell £10,000 worth of goods that month to make a £2,000 profit. If you're running a service and your margins are say 50%, you've got to sell £4,000 worth of services to make your £2,000. And that's just to make your gross profit.

"It's vital that you work out your target earnings and then your required sales target to meet those earnings!"

Getting Started

Remember that your "takeaway" or net profit is the difference between sales less purchases and the other costs of doing business, such as overheads, and other expenses etc.

So, you need to start with these numbers. And this is where your pricing starts to come into play. Now, there's a number of things you can do. You can sell more products, or you can sell more services, or you can up your fees. You get to choose.

Either way, it's absolutely vital that you work out what you need to earn down to the daily rate. If you need to make £100, then you need to sell on a consistent basis enough product or enough service to give you that net profit of £100. You need to know your numbers.

It's at this point that business owners often get a bit nervous, because they worry that the amount they need to charge to generate their minimum required net profit is too high and that will put off potential customers. But, as explained below, the issue for most potential customers isn't usually price, but quality and value for money.

Ultimately, and always bear this in mind: the biggest problem with price is usually between your ears - your own mindset! It's not necessarily an issue for your customers.

So how do you set the price?

Let's come back to pricing itself. One of the first things that you need to get into your head is that pricing is rarely about the pound or the dollar amount. Pricing is usually about the value that you bring to the market. Now, let me

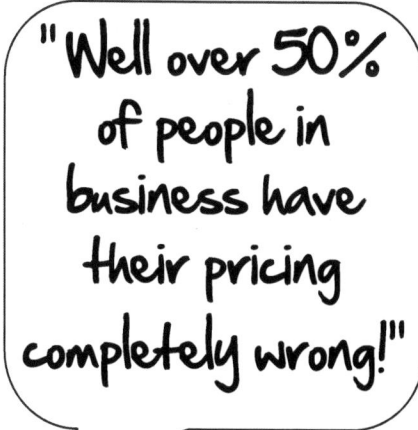

"Well over 50% of people in business have their pricing completely wrong!"

explain what I mean. If price was the only reason people bought something, luxury companies like Rolex, BMW and Prada would have been long gone.

But, the pricing often isn't the issue. The pricing is usually secondary to the value you bring.

So, what do we do about bringing value? Well, the first thing we need to do is to look at what you do for your customers. Like I said, if you sell jewellery, are you going to make your customers look good and feel fantastic? Because ultimately, when somebody buys jewellery, that's what they're after. They're not usually after just another trinket. They want to look good and feel good. It's a luxury buy and this is actually what you're selling to them. And, if that wasn't the case, companies that sell jewellery, like Tiffany's, would have been out of business a long time ago. Okay. So, **it's not always about the price; it's about what you do for the customers and their perception of the value of your good or services.**

Now, here's a very important point. Don't compare yourself to your competition because your competition will be out there scrambling for the same number of customers and, in a lot of cases, they'll all be dropping their prices. Price comparison can be a useful approach, especially when you're starting out. And, in my experience, well over 50% of people in business have their pricing wrong and almost all business owners worry about their pricing more than their customers do. So, don't compare yourself to competition simply because it's likely that over half of them are wrong about where they pitch their pricing. Focus on value. Don't think about your competitors.

What about price comparison?

Another important thing to consider is, don't rely too heavily on competing on price. And the reason is: it is a fast race to the bottom. In my experience, those who compete on price don't tend to last or they work very hard for not a lot of return. Unless you've got a mass-produced and mass-shipped product, selling on price is going to lead to hard work and low (or no) profit. Trust me, I've been there, done that and it's not pretty or fun. So, don't compete on price. If you've got people coming to you saying, "Well, I can get it cheaper down the street," you've got a choice. You can either say, "Well, you know what? You get what you pay for. Feel free to go down the street." Or, you can do the next thing, which is to try and add some value.

When low pricing is too low...

So, with that lot in mind, I'd like to divert slightly and tell you a little bit of a story about my website design business. We sell websites and additional web marketing services. When I started the company, I charged just a few hundred pounds for a website, which was dirt cheap. Interestingly enough, I did get some customers. But, considering the amount of work that goes into a website, I quickly realized that there was a limit to what I could physically produce for the money. Thus the number of projects I could physically do was limited, which meant that I had an earnings limit. I wasn't charging a lot for a website and it would take me anywhere between five and ten working days to build a website. Then, I realized that I was working for below minimum wage. So, I had to do something about it.

I mentioned this to a very good friend of mine who is a business coach and she told me, "You're too cheap and you need to double your fees." I was a little unnerved by this but I thought, "Okay. I'll double my fee. I'll make my websites £1,000 each." Still not too expensive, but it's a little bit further away from the bargain basement prices I was

> "Higher prices are likely to be more of a problem for you than they are for customers!"

charging.

So, the next time I went to visit a potential customer, I sat in front of her, and she said, "How much is it?" I simply said, "It's £1,000." And she said, "Okay. Let's do it." At that point, I nearly fell off my chair because *I was so worried about having more than doubled my fees.* I was worried about whether anyone was ever going to buy from me. In all honesty, the high price problem was only between my ears.

What I also did was to add value to the offering. I added things into the package. So, instead of just building a website, we included additional SEO to help their websites perform better in the search engines. We also added some coaching on how to manage and promote their website as well. I added value to the proposition and automatically doubled my income.

Now, it's a gutsy thing to do and I know that, if you sell jewellery, doubling your prices is going to be very hard work. And if you sell a price sensitive product like cars or food, doubling your prices just isn't feasible. But, that's what happened to me.

But the big lesson for me was that **the pricing problem was my problem and not my customers' problem**. Because, if you pitch it right and you've built up that value proposition, people will pay what you ask as long as it's considered a fair and reasonable price.

A really good example of widely varying prices is ladies underwear. You can buy underwear for just a few pounds a time or you can pay hundreds. Does paying hundreds mean that you're getting better clothes? Not always. Even the big-name designer labels have their clothes made at similar costs (and sometimes even in the same sweatshops) to the mass-produced retailers. The key thing here is the perception of quality and value, and that perception dictates the price.

So, think about what I did, **I doubled my fee and added value**. I do not ever compete on price these days. I never even contemplate it. I do get people saying to me, "I can get this thing done for a third of what you're asking down the street." My response is usually, "Okay. Well, you better go down the street and get it. But I promise that you'll struggle to find a better deal." What I found interesting is that some people end up coming back to me later to have the job done properly, and then they pay what I'm asking.

> "If you want to charge a higher price then you need to increase the value offering of your product or service!"

Now, another great way to get your pricing right is to **think about incrementally raising your prices** until you start to get some price resistance. This is a great way of getting your pricing right. That's what we've been doing over the last couple of years in my website design business. We're over 200% more expensive than when we started because, after we doubled our prices, we've incrementally increasing our prices to see at what point our market will stand.

The point is, we want to provide good value for money which is usually not directly related to the price. We want to provide great value to the point where our clients will tell people about what we do and they'll rave about us when we ask them for a testimonial.

It's all about fairness and value. We strive for that in our business and we encourage our clients to think the same way. If BMW wasn't perceived as value for money, no one would buy from them. Yes, you get the prestige of driving a luxury car, but there's still value. If it was outrageously priced, chances are good very few people would buy them. So, think about value for money.

The power of supersizing

Now, another great thing about being self-employed is that you have the flexibility to try stuff like premium offerings and upgrades.

> "Look for ways to develop your own premium product or service. If it's there someone will buy it!"

Most of us have been to McDonalds and have been asked if we would like to Supersize it or 'go large' with that order. When McDonalds first introduced this, every single front of house staff was trained to ask that question. All you get is more fries and more soda, which costs them pennies to produce. But, the upshot of asking that question was that it added just over 17% to McDonalds' profitability just for asking the question "Would you like to go large with that?"

So, my question to you is: can you develop a premium product or premium service?

Can you do something in your business, so that every time somebody wants to buy something, you say, "Would you like to go large with that?" And, if you sell jewellery for example, could you say, "There's some beautiful earrings here. Would you like to add a matching necklace for this 'wonderfully advantageous' price for buying the earrings?"

If you sell legal services for example, is there a way of adding value to the proposition? If you sell a will-writing service, is there something you can add on top for an advantageous price when somebody's hot and they're really into buying from you?

Getting Started

Offer different price points

In our website design business, we have three price points - a basic, standard, and top-of-the-range price. The basic package, like I said, is over 3 times what we used to charge for a website. The next one up is about a third more than that, which has added marketing, and SEO, and support. And with the top package, we just do everything. We build the website, do loads of online marketing, provide coaching and loads more. Our top product is nearly twice the price of the lowest priced package. Interestingly enough, over 50% of our clients buy the middle package. They buy the middle priced package because we've added a load of value on top. You get additional marketing, some extra SEO, online promotion for your business, write some blog posts and more.

So, is there a package you can offer that enables you to ask your customers, "Would you like to go large with that?" I would be very surprised if there's no way you could offer an upgrade. Amazon is a great example. "People who bought this also bought that." And, interestingly enough, large numbers of people buy 'that' as well as this, simply because it's there. Amazon don't publish the numbers but if it wasn't profitable they simply wouldn't do it.

> "Over 50% of our clients buy an upgraded service, just because it's there. If we didn't offer it nobody would buy it!"

If you don't offer the upgrade, people can't buy it!

I didn't start asking people to upgrade. I started writing it on the proposals. Every single proposal went out with an upgrade price and people started buying it, just because it's there. If it's never there, they'll never buy. Have a think about that.

So, next time you're shopping online with any of the big retailers, they'll always be offering you an upgrade. "Would you like this for an advantageous price?" It's very common now and it's very easy to do in almost any business. As a good example, I bought a car recently. I was asked if I wanted to buy an extended warranty which is really just an insurance policy. But, it's an upgrade price. It would have added, if I'd bought it, an extra few percent to the price of the deal and would have been a great, instant, easy earner for the guy selling the car.

So, have a think. Are there ways you can offer an upgraded price, an upgraded package, an upgraded anything in your business so that you're giving everybody who buys from you the opportunity to spend some more money?

Payment plans

Now, another big thing on price that's made a big difference for us as well is that we sell packaged products. Now, because we're dealing in thousands of pounds instead of just a few hundred, we offer **payment plans** to all of our customers. They can pay for their new website over 3 months or they can pay for it over 6 months. And, if they pay for it over 6 months, it costs them a little bit more because we are financing that product.

Interestingly enough, 50% of our clients go for the 6-month option, which automatically adds an extra 8% to the sale price. Yes, we take a hit in the short-term cash flow, but what would have been a product worth about £1,500 suddenly costs them just over £1,600 because they opted for a payment plan.

"Payment plans are a great way to get over price objections on bigger ticket items!"

Getting Started

So, how about offering some kind of payment plan? If you sell a big-ticket item, simply say, "Well, I can put you on a direct debit payment plan, an automatic standing order payment plan for the next 6 or 12 months to pay for it." Can you do that? Is that feasible for your business?

If you sell bigger ticket items, it certainly takes the price objection out of the mind of the customers. Very rarely does anybody go buy a £20,000 car and pay cash. Almost always, they will finance it. Why? Because not many folks have £20,000 just lying around to be spent on a car. But, they'll be able to afford a few hundred pounds a month. And even though you think you're getting a zero interest deal, the price almost always includes an arrangement fee for the dealer, so they still make a decent profit out of doing it. So, think about whether you can do this. Can you offer financing or payment plans?

One thing to be aware of though: if you're offering finance to consumers in the UK you'll likely need a Consumer Credit License. So make sure you check this out before offering payment terms to consumers.

And, finally -- and this is a big one for all small businesses -- **if you're too busy, you're probably too cheap.**

Being inundated with work is an indicator that you're probably a little too cheap. If you win every single project, or every single customer that you pitch at, you're probably too cheap.

I have a friend, Tim, he's our plumber and he's constantly over-busy. Literally, he could work 12 hours a day, seven days a week and still not keep up with the demand for him and what he does. I've been telling him for ages; "You're too cheap."

Now he did admit that he was scared to up his prices but

I suggested, "Well, if you put your prices up by 10%, who's going to hurt?" And he said, "Well, I might lose some clients." And I said, "Well, if you put your prices up by 10% and lose 10% of your clients, what have you lost? You've lost 10% of your customers but you've not really lost any money."

That's a very common thing in business. If Tim puts his prices up by 10%, he's probably still going to be just as in demand, but he's just going to be earning a little bit more money, which means he might be able to take a holiday here and there.

So, let's put it all together.

Start with what you need to earn. Work that down to a per-hour or a per-product amount and work out how much you need to sell. It always starts there. Always think about then how you can price yourself to earn that kind of money. If it's not enough, you need to sell more, which means you need to deliver more or you need to adjust your pricing. To be honest, you could probably do a combination of the two.

> "If you're too busy then it's possible that you're too cheap!"

Next, make sure you try and **increase the value of what you offer**. It's actually easier than you might think to sell more expensive products and services, especially when the value proposition has been well pitched.

Think about how you might be able to up-sell what you offer. **Can you add a premium product** or a go-large?

Remember - if you sell bigger ticket items, offer the clients the chance to pay for it over a number of months. But remember, the **financing can take away pricing fears** but it should never be free - you should always add a charge for providing the facility.

And finally, remember: you probably worry about pricing much more than your customers. Pricing is all about value for money, not cost and that's where you need to start.

Chapter 4
Getting Those First Few Customers

One of the difficulties about being self-employed, when you first start, is that most people start with zero customers. Of course, you've just set up on your own, you're all excited, and you're ready to hit the road. You've got a great idea, you think your product (or service) is going to do well and everyone's going to want to buy it, etc.

Unfortunately, having **a brilliant product or service isn't worth much until you have customers**. But finding customers isn't always as easy as it looks. Some people are actually very nervous about selling and some people have no idea how to do it. Very few of us are natural sales people. So the best way of doing it is to see it as a process with a series of steps from identifying potential customers to closing those very first sales.

A lot of people seem to think that they need to go out and reinvent the marketing and sales wheel to win those first customers. And it's just not the case. **It's all about using the resources you have at your fingertips.**

"Start with the people you know, always!"

So I'd like to give you some thoughts on how you can make those first few contacts and hopefully, in a very short, time rustle up some business and get some cash flowing.

Where do you start?

Typically, and this is an often overlooked element of being self-employed, you should always **start with those people you already know**.

Network marketing business, like Amway, Forever Living or Avon, always tell new agents to write a long list of all the people you know. They expect you to go through that list and contact them and talk to them about the business opportunity and the products that you're now offering. And the principle is exactly the same when you're self-employed, whether you're selling business-to-business or to retail customers.

So, I've developed a list of what you can do to get those first few customers.

Friends and Family

So, first off, friends and family. In Britain we always seem a bit reluctant to talk to friends and family if we run a business, and ask for help. I don't know why, but we Brits just don't like talking about money or business.

Well, I say, "Screw that." When you're self-employed you can't afford to think like that any more. You're in business. You're in business to make a profit. Maybe not to make a fortune, but certainly to make a living, and there's no reason why you shouldn't ask friends and family to recommend people or to give you some names of people they work with or they know who you can add to your list of contacts. All you're doing is asking them a favour.

If you wanted to borrow their car for a day, you'd have no problem. Or, if you wanted them to babysit the kids, you'd probably have no problem asking. And they'd have no problems asking you for a favour. So, ask them to do you this little bit of favour and think if they can do anything to help you find customers.

Your network of friends

You can also **ask friends about their friends**. Do they know someone in a particular company that you might want to do business with? Don't be afraid to do that leveraging, that networking.

The next one is **people you went to school with**, if it's fairly recent, or people you went to university with. A lot of people who go to university go on to start businesses. Have you been in touch with them? Could you get in touch with them?

A lot of universities have alumni associations and have regular networking events. They run reunions. Do you go to these? Have you met people you used to go to school with lately, spoken to them, been in touch with them? Again, ask them. It's definitely worth getting in touch.

Business Connections

Now, the chances are good also that you have **business connections**. Now, this could be former employees. It could be an employer. It could be somebody you used to work with or work for.

Now, as long as left your last employer on fairly good terms and you're not going into direct competition with them, there's nothing wrong with going back and asking them whether you can do some work for them or, potentially, do some work for some of their customers or contacts. Again, if you left on good terms, you could end up with a very beneficial business relationship, assuming you are selling business-to-business.

But, even if you're selling to consumers, the chances are good

Getting Started

you have a very wide market. So don't be afraid to talk to people, those you used to work with and those who you used to work for.

Outside of work

The next stop is **what do you do outside of work**? What are you involved in? Are you involved in a sports club? Are you involved in some kind of social club? Do you go to a church? Are you a member of any kind of civic organization? It could be the Rotary. Do you do any volunteering anywhere? Do any members of your family do any volunteering anywhere?

> "Don't forget those you know socially. They could help to introduce you to potential clients!"

Again, it's leveraging those you know in the groups that you're in with a view to asking them a huge favour to help you get your business off the ground. And the chances are good, even if you sell business-to-business and you want to do business with a local firm, it's highly likely that someone you know either knows somebody who works in there or has worked there in the past. So, never be afraid to ask.

Trade Organisations

Do you belong to any **trade or professional** organisations? Have you ever belonged to a trade group in the past? Is there a database you can tap into there? Do you know tradespeople?

Chances are good you've used a plumber, possibly even a lawyer, maybe even a doctor, a dentist, insurance agent, a hairstylist, a mechanic, you might even know a babysitter.

Think about all of the people you've done business with in the past, can they help you? Can you ask them for their help or if they're interested in trying out what it is you're buying or selling? It's always good to get feedback from other business owners. The worst thing that can happen is that they say "no". And, as a business owner, you have to get used to that word!

Finally what about the professional advisors you've used for your personal affairs? For example, when you bought your house? It could be an estate agent. It could be the bank manager. It could be a lawyer, a mortgage advisor, a builder -- all of these people are either potential customers or know people who could be potential customers

Neighbours, past neighbours and your extended family

It's also worth talking to neighbours and past neighbours. And, of course, then you've got your partner's friends and family. Don't just rely on yours. The chances are good that your partner, if you have one, knows a lot of people as well. You might be a bit nervous about asking for help, but it's certainly worth trying to tap into your extended circle to get a start on your list.

And finally, what about your online contacts?

Even if you just networked with people on Facebook, even if you just know them through LinkedIn, chances are good that you know hundreds of people. So, you should be able to put together quite a substantial list from what I've just told you.

So, now you've got your list of potential customers. What do you do next?

Getting Started

Step One: Get your "hot list"

The first thing is to narrow that list down into potentially good contacts - a "hot list" of potential clients. Are they potential buyers first of all of what you have to offer? Or could they be a referrer of business by introducing you to a potential buyer?

If you know somebody who works for a bank (for example) and you want to sell training services to large organizations, then finding out through your contact who the training manager or training director is would be a useful start. So, narrow this list down to potential customers.

The next step is to narrow the list down to people who know potential customers. It could well be that you know someone who works in a bank and you want to do business with that bank, then they know a potential customer.

If you want to work with plumbers, but you don't know a plumber, chances are good a builder you've done business with in the past will know a plumber. So, they know potential customers. So, again, write down that list, and make that list, and do that.

So, what do we do with this newly developed list? The thing is to **narrow down a hot list**.

Step Two: Make contact!

Once you've identified your potential customers in your target market, then refine the list and split it into as many demographic groups for your target market as you can identify. Narrow those down first. Break them down into chunks. If there's a large

"You're looking to build a 'hot list' of potential clients!"

group of these people, a large list, then break them down into manageable chunks of maybe 25.

The reason is because you're going to send them a personal letter and follow-up to try and generate interest.

This sounds like a time-consuming exercise and it is. If you send out hundreds of letters and you are planning on following up with all those people, it's going to be a big job. But you don't have to do it all at once; identify your best prospects and start with them first.

Make it personal

What you do is to send out a personal letter to all of these people telling them that you've just started in business. Offer them a free consultation, or a free sample of what it is you're doing, or a special discount, just something to get their interest.

All you're trying to do in the minute is pique their interest. Get them to raise their head and say, "Hey, you know what, this looks interesting." Nothing more than that. You're not trying to sell them anything. All you're doing is trying to get some interest.

The key then is to follow up.

You've got to follow up. How you follow up is up to you, but the most important thing is that you keep reminding people that you exist and that you're there to help them. Eventually, some of them will be interested.

You could follow up on the phone. That's often a good idea and particularly if you're selling high value goods or services - you need to speak directly to the potential buyer if it's at all possible. If you're going to call, you want to make sure that you put in your letter that you'll be giving them a call within a few days and then do exactly that. Don't leave it more than a couple of days though, people are busy and memories fade.

For many people, making a telephone call is the most difficult step of all, because you actually have to talk directly to your potential customers. It's not easy talking to a stranger at the best of times, more so when you're trying to sell something. But you could always follow up with another letter, or an email. Just do something!

Organise your follow up

As I explained at the start of the chapter, **the key to finding customers is to do it as a process**. The follow up is a very important part of that process. Typically, when we send out sales letters in our business, we post them out on Monday and we follow up on Wednesday and Thursday simply because you want to catch people while the idea is still in their mind if they've read your letter.

"always, Always, ALWAYS follow up. The key to success in sales is to follow up!"

A lot of people won't read your letter, you just have to accept that, that's the way the game is. But, always follow up. Find out if they read your letter, what their initial thoughts were, and whether you could actually go and see them or potentially help them with something in the short term.

Remember, you're giving them a special offer or a discount. You'll give them a free sample, a special free consultation, something to get that relationship and that ball rolling.

Another great thing to do is **follow up some more**. Add

people to a CRM system (more on that later) if you have their email addresses. I hope you do. Then, send them something in an email a week later. Just keep up the process.

And, then, what you do is you start to set up short meetings, and you go to these meetings, and you talk to them about what you do to see if there is some way that you can work together.

Now, what I've just done is outlined a very simple direct sales strategy.

You have to make a start and this is as good a way as any. Finding customers may not come naturally to you, but you have to do it and get used to doing it. You're going to have to send out some emails. You're going to have to pick up the phone. You're going to have to have some meetings and discussions with people. And the more you do it, the easier it becomes.

But, if you get good at this stuff, you will never go hungry. If you get good at this sales process and refine it, and improve it, and learn the numbers -- and I'll cover that in a different section -- then you will know exactly how many letters you have to send out, and exactly how many calls you have to make, how many follow-ups you have to do, how many meetings do you have to have to meet your sales and turnover target. It really can become scientific once you do this.

"80% of small businesses don't have a consistent sales and marketing plan. Aim to be in the other 20%!"

Getting Started

Here's an interesting thing: 80% of small businesses won't go through this process. 80% of small businesses won't have a consistent approach to their sales and marketing. You want to put yourself in that top 20%. If you want to reap 80% of the rewards from your industry in terms of comparing yourself to your competition, then do this. It isn't complex, but it isn't easy.

I'll be covering a more in-depth sales and marketing process in a later chapter but always start with what and who you know. Make a start and make it happen.

Chapter 5
What to Do on Your First Day

Some of you reading this book will already be up and running your own businesses. But if you're just starting out, that "first" day can be anything from nerve-wracking to exciting to downright over-whelming! There's so much to do and you need to know where to start.

So what DO you do on your first day of being self-employed? This depends on whether you're starting from scratch, or if you've already made a start on the "background" stuff. Perhaps you've built a website, or you've found your retail premises, or you've started a marketing campaign. Either way, the end goal is the same - to sell your goods or services to customers, so your "first day" should be focused on that long term goal.

First of all: tell EVERYBODY you're "OPEN FOR BUSINESS"!

You'll never get any customers if people don't know that you're open for business, so the first thing is to tell absolutely everybody you're open for business! Make a noise about it, whether you're trading online or retail, or if you're a service business.

Just tell everyone. Don't be shy. Don't be too British about it - get out there and make a noise!

> "Everything you do your first day should be aimed at getting customers as quickly as possible!"

Getting Started

If you're opening a new shop or restaurant or hairdressers, you need to make a bit of a splash in the local neighbourhood.

Do a leaflet campaign in the local area (a good way to help teenage children earn their pocket money!), meet your neighbouring retailers and ask if you can put a poster in their window, put a BIG advert in your local paper. You also want an online presence so that if somebody types "hardware stores in Nottingham", your name pops up on every search engine.

If you're a **service provider - a consultant, an accountant, a solicitor - you need to get the message out to prospective clients, whether it's a personalised letter, email**, something that will make them sit up and take notice that you're available for business.

If you're starting an **online business, you need to start your online marketing campaigns so that people know that you're open for business**. Read the chapters about Finding your first few customers, Marketing and Selling - there are loads of ideas to help you find prospective customers, both traditional and online. Get your search engine campaign underway on your website, Twitter, LinkedIn, Facebook, Instagram; **start posting about the exciting news of your new venture**.

Make sure that your website is functioning and up-to-date, with latest information, e.g. your opening hours and contact details. Write a blog post about opening your doors for business.

Tell everybody because **even if they don't buy, they may know some people who might**. So spread the word and ask everybody to tell everybody they know - it's all about numbers!

Go out and literally tell the world that you're open for business!

Getting customers

So now that you've told **everyone you're open for business, pretty much everything you do must be aimed at getting customers** as quickly as possible. How you do that largely depends on the type of business.

If you're a retailer, you might start with an opening party where customers can come and get a discount and a small free gift just for coming into the shop. A party is also a great idea for a restaurant or bar; find something that fits your type of business and will appeal to your prospective customers.

If you're selling to businesses and you have to meet people to sell your goods or services, you need to find ways to get in front of those people with whom you'd like to do business. Aim at those first few appointments. A good thing we always recommend is to send out an email to as many people as possible, including all of your contacts, not just prospective clients, to let them know that you're open for business. And, if you've already identified prospective clients, you can start by sending out say some personalised letters on that first day - maybe ten letters - then following up with phone calls a few days later with a view to making appointments.

> "When you're self-employed, time really IS money!"

Being disciplined

Whatever type of business you're opening, the first few days always feel a bit strange and it's easy to become distracted

Getting Started

with everything that's going on and your never-ending "to-do" list. So you need to be as disciplined as you possibly can with your time and get into good working habits.

Either way, you don't want to waste too much time – when you're self-employed, time really IS money!

On my first day, I tried doing everything apart from facing up to the fact that I actually had to do something. I was the boss and I had no one looking over my shoulder telling me what to do. It's surprisingly difficult if you don't actually have a plan of action to begin with. Thankfully, I managed to get into some networking events fairly quickly, and that's how I developed my contact database, and that's how I ultimately identified potential clients and developed my sales. The faster you can get into your marketing channels, the better, whether it's online or in person.

If you're starting from scratch, then your first day could also be a planning day, where you just get the ball rolling in some way. Start setting things up. Start making appointments. Start getting out to events. Start banging out on your social media that you're open for business. Start sending out emails if you've already got a list.

> "Make a plan, be productive, start as you mean to go on!"

The important thing is this: *just do something that helps your business. Don't sit on your hands. Don't waste time*. The key to starting out as self-employed is to get momentum as fast as you can and to keep that ball rolling. You want to start off being as productive as possible during your first few days because it helps you to develop that momentum.

Do whatever you need to do to help you focus on your business. You might find it helps if you wear your "work" clothes, because it helps to feel business-like and in a working environment. Make sure that your working environment is free from distractions because that can also be a major problem, especially if you work from home. Use the spare room and keep the door closed to avoid domestic distractions when you're working. Or go to a local coffee shop for a few hours, the library, somewhere with Wi-Fi so you can do something productive.

The key, as Burt Burton (founder of 4N) said, is to "do something, anything that contributes to your business." Either way, be excited about it! Make the most of that "shiny new business" feeling and enjoy the process! Make a plan, be productive, start as you mean to go on.

Chapter 6
Looking After the Money - Financial Planning and Managing Money

In this chapter, I'd like to cover an area which many people get wrong. It's all about money and financial management. The problem with this particular topic is, if you get it wrong, the consequences can be quite serious. So I'm going to discuss some very practical and common-sense pointers to help you avoid getting into a mess with your finances.

Getting professional help

One of the things that you need to be aware of right up front is that, at least in the UK, you're not obliged to have an accountant to do your accounts or to even do your tax return. You do need to keep records but you also don't need to have an overbearing and complicated accounting system. **So keep it as simple as possible to begin with**.

However, what I do recommend is that you find yourself a good bookkeeper. Many bookkeepers in the UK are skilled enough to be able to keep your records up to date, produce some financial reports, run a payroll, and also help you with your tax return and company returns.

"You don't need an accountant but I recommend you get a book-keeper!"

So do some research, preferably get a few recommendations from others in your business community.

What you'll find is that an accountant will be considerably more expensive than a bookkeeper. And it's highly likely that an accountant add no more value to your business than a bookkeeper would. So bear that in mind.

But there are good reasons for having an accountant, for example if you need help with and financial planning and business development advice. They can be quite expensive to begin with, but they should add value to your business by helping you with good financial advice.

Legal Compliance

Whether or not you pay for professional help, one of the most important things to do right from the start is to make sure that you've got all your compliance boxes ticked. To start with, get a business bank account, always a good idea. Even if you don't have a limited company, (an incorporated company), it's often a good idea to get a bank account in your business name.

> "Sounds boring but you need to make sure you tick all the compliance boxes!"

Make sure that you've notified the tax authorities that you are self-employed or running a small business because they will need to know and they will need to set up their systems for you to provide the necessary tax returns. It's important to do this in advance so that you don't end up having to pay penalties for late notification, e.g. if you register for VAT later than you should.

Getting Started

Make sure you've also bought the appropriate insurances according to what you need. If you have an office, you'll need public liability. If you have staff, you'll need employer's liability as well. If you sell goods by distance, you'll probably need transit, or shipping insurance, or other things like this. So do your research and make sure you've got the right insurances. I know it can be an expense upfront, but it's better to be safe than sorry should something go wrong.

Cashflow

So first things first, one of the biggest things for you to do, no matter how well you're doing in your business, is to keep an eye on cash flow. Many self-employed people underestimate the importance of this. They just assume that, if business is going and money is flowing, that things are all okay.

> "Keep an eye on cash-flow and don't let anyone owe you money for too long!"

But, if you don't keep an eye on cash, you could end up in a position where you're working away, with money is coming in and money is going out, but you don't actually know if you're making a profit. So keep an eye on the cash flow. Get regular feedback on what your cash position and your profit position is like.

This is where a bookkeeper can really come into their own and earn their weight by enabling you to see your profit picture on a regular basis. And you should be having a look at least once a month to make sure that you're still making a profit. To begin with, you probably won't make much, if any, profit in the first year. But, as things start flowing and business starts going, then you need to know how much money is coming into the business and whether you're making any profit.

If you're not making any money, you want to be able to quickly do something about it.

Credit control

One of the things I also recommend is to make sure that you're operation a proper credit control system. The last thing you need is a customer to owe you money for ages without you being aware that they haven't paid. Put a proper system in place to monitor your accounts receivable so that you can follow up outstanding bills and ask clients to pay outstanding debts.

> "You don't have to give 30 days credit so keep your credit terms as tight as possible!"

You also need to monitor your own debts to avoid building up a backlog or debts and to get a true picture of your business's cash position.

In our website design business, we send out invoices for hosting and we give people no credit terms. In other words, we expect them to pay as soon as they receive the invoice. We certainly don't give 30 days. No one is obliged to give 30 days' credit and you shouldn't too. Always make sure your terms and conditions are good, though, and that people you do business with understand that these are your payment terms. And make sure that they agree with them usually via an email, or in writing, or something like that. You might also want to request a deposit for large projects or from new clients.

In many ways, and I appreciate that this depends on the type of business you're in and the type of clients you have, but you never should give lengthy credit terms. In doing this you're, ultimately, becoming a financier for your clients. Small businesses, the self-employed, and start-ups just can't afford to be a bank. You can't afford to give interest-free loans to clients because they take ages to pay. So make sure your credit control is good. Make sure that, if you're going to give credit terms, you keep it short.

Terms and conditions

My lawyer, Marie, told me off when I was giving 30 days' credit and people were paying in 40 - 50 days, and then I was wondering why I had a cash flow issue. She said, "No. Payment in seven days or you're on the phone asking why they've not coughed up." And this is important because it's your cash that your clients are hanging onto, so don't let them get away with it.

This is where your terms and conditions really come into their own as well. Make sure your terms and conditions are fit for purpose. If possible, get them checked over by a lawyer, preferably a friend who will do it for next to nothing. This is because, like I said, you cannot afford to finance other people's business operations. You're not a charity and you need a profit to make so you should be on top of it regularly.

Dealing with tax payments

Now another important thing is tax, whether it's income tax, corporation tax or VAT. At some point, you will have to pay tax. Interestingly enough, most tax authorities don't necessarily expect small businesses and the self-employed to make a profit in the first couple of years. In fact, they're often surprised when businesses do make a profit and end up paying tax in their first year. So don't panic if you haven't actually made a profit and you haven't actually got a tax bill. That's not unusual.

However, if you are in a positive cash position and you look like you're going to be paying tax, then you need to do something with it. What I always recommend is that you put away 10% of your turnover or at least 10% of your profit each month into a savings account to save up for the potential tax bill. I know that 10% might sound like a lot, especially if money is tight, but to be honest, chances are good you won't end up paying that much, which will give a little bit of money in the bank. But it's always good to know that, if you get a tax bill, you've got most, if not all of it, already covered. I've been there, done that, and panicking about being able to afford the tax bill isn't funny at all. So plan for it, build a contingency into your business, put money aside on a very regular basis. So, when the tax man sends you a bill, you should have money in the bank and it shouldn't be such a shock to the system.

> "Regularly putting money aside for your tax bill is a good idea!"

If you're registered for VAT, keep the VAT on your sales in your business account so that it's available to pay HMRC every three months. It's easy to fall into the "default" (i.e. penalty) system with VAT because you normally have to submit and pay 4 returns each year, so try to keep your VAT money separate so that you can pay it on time.

Accounting system

Also, one of the things that a lot of people misunderstand is their accounting system. You don't have to have a complex accounting system. There's loads of online accounting systems like Xero. They are pretty good.

Getting Started

In all honesty, we run our accounting for our website design business on a spreadsheet, albeit a rather large spreadsheet. Depending on your business you don't really need anything more complex than that. We don't send out a huge number of invoices because most of our clients go on some kind of direct debit system. So we're not normally waiting for money. As a result, we don't need a complex accounting system and, thus far, we've managed to do it all on a spreadsheet.

But if you have large numbers of transactions, you NEED a decent accounting system. If you sell retail, either e-commerce or in a shop, it's a good idea to have some kind of stock control hooked up to your accounting system. That's just sensible stuff. But, if you have a services business, you probably don't need anything more than a simple sales and purchase accounts. Your bookkeeper or accountant will be able to help you decide on the best type of system for your business. Either way, keep it as simple as you possibly can and make sure that system gives you regular feedback as to whether you're making any money. Remember that profit and cash-flow are separate issues: you need to understand your cash position so that you know whether or not you're making any profit!

"Keep your accounting system as simple as possible!"

What about paying yourself?

This is an important thing and it's the reason we're doing this thing. Many business gurus will recommend paying yourself before you pay anybody else because, otherwise, there is no point in being in business. If you're self-employed and you don't have a limited company, you don't need a payroll because everything you earn goes into your account and you are the business. So you don't need to run a payroll to pay yourself. So your net profit, based on what you've earned, will be what you pay tax on and it will be your personal taxation through the self-assessment (in the UK) tax return system.

If you trade through a limited (incorporated) company, then you've got the option to pay yourself with payroll. It will cost you a little bit to administer, but you also then maximize the tax deduction of a payroll on your business to save on the company's tax bill. You also then maximize your own tax benefits by paying yourself as much as you possibly can tax-free through your tax code as an employee of the company. Again, a good bookkeeper should be able to help you with this. Just make sure you notify the tax authorities that this is the position. To be honest, if you keep it simple, and make sure that you're managing and watching the money, you shouldn't really get into financial problems through lack of record keeping.

Of course, just having a good accounting system won't guarantee that your business will make a profit. If you're not selling enough to cover your costs or you're not selling enough to make a profit, that's a different issue and you need to rethink your sales and marketing strategy. But you shouldn't get into problems because of lack of financial management. Trust me, the tax authorities are never very sympathetic when you owe them a load of money and simply tell them, "I'm sorry, but I didn't know that I was going to have a big tax bill." It never, ever goes down well.

So the key points are:
- keep it simple,
- make sure you know what cash-flow position you're in,
- put money aside for tax,
- **and make sure you're up-to-date with credit control.**

Chapter 7
Being Organised And Coping With Overwhelming Workloads

One of the things that a lot of the self-help gurus tend to overlook is the fact that, when you run a small business or you are self-employed, there can often be an immense feeling of being **overwhelmed by the sheer volume of stuff that you need to do**.

To be honest, I've been running small businesses most of my adult life with varying degrees of success and the feeling never really goes away. There really is too much to do and never enough time available to do it. And, when you're running a small business or running you as a small business, there is never nothing to do. You could theoretically work 24 hours a day 7 days a week and still not feel like you've got everything done.

So, the key then is to **work out some plans or some strategies for tackling this feeling and to make your own life so much easier**. As I've said in another part of the book, I always try and plan my work as much as I possibly can.

I do marketing almost every single day. I aim at an hour. I call it the "Marketing Power Hour." Sometimes, it's 30 minutes; sometimes it's 90 minutes; the average is

"The day's not over until the next day's planned!"

somewhere between 45 and 60 minutes almost every single day.

Why? Because I know that the success of my business, the long-term sustainability of my business, depends on my ability to get and keep customers. So, for me, that's not a negotiable thing unless I'm out of the office and physically can't do that.

So, what do we do to begin to organize ourselves and tackle the sheer volume of stuff to do? Well, first things first. **You need to write yourself a to-do list, and I always think that the best place to start is to write tomorrow's to-do list today**. If you start living by the phrase, "The day's not over until the next day is planned," you'll have a better idea of what you're meant to be doing when you hit your desk in the morning because there's nothing that wastes times and puts you into things which are not productive faster than not knowing what to do when you get to your desk.

I have a very good friend who says, "Well, I've got my to-do list in my mind." To be honest, I've said it to her and I would say this to anybody, **"Don't trust your memory."**

I hate to say it, but *your mind is one of the most unreliable memory stores out* there because it's easily distracted by other things. So, write it down. I don't care who you are, how organized you think you are, how great you think your memory is, write it down. There is no better way. When it's on paper, believe it or not, it reinforces your memory even more. So, your mind becomes that little bit more reliable. Get it down on paper.

Plan tomorrow today. When you do that, you can write down a list of things that need to be done or you're aiming to get done. Write yourself a series of numbers beside each point in terms of their priority. Some of them will be fun, some of them not so fun. The key is to try to get a balance of things that are important and things that are a little more enjoyable, but for the long term. You decide how to organize what's important. I can't prescribe it to you, but it's up to you to make it happen.

So, write stuff down. Have a weekly plan if necessary. "By the end of this week, I want to achieve X" and then each day schedule in time to get it done. So, you don't have to do it all in a single block, especially if it's not a fun thing. You can literally do some of it every day which means that your deadline will happen.

Here's another point, a very important one: deadlines. **Set deadlines for things**. The reason why is that deadlines tend to get things done. The old phrase, "I'll do it when I get around to it," I'm sure we've all done that before and how often do we get around to it? Typically, we don't. So, set deadlines for as much as you possibly can and then make sure you put in time to get the deadline stuff done.

As I've said, there's always going to be too many things to juggle. So, you need to find your own time-management or self-management techniques.

If you genuinely have too much to do, then you need to start thinking slightly differently. So, you need to start cutting out things which don't produce a result for you, like going on social media every hour of every day.

Give yourself time and space

One of the things that works well for me *if I need to focus on something is I switch off my phone and I switch off my email*. Believe it or not, despite the fact that I'm not connected to the rest of the world, no one dies. Customers don't rant and rave. I don't get fired by people I'm working for. My suppliers don't panic. Nothing happens. When you switch off your phone and your email for the sake of focus, no one will suffer.

You might think, **"Yeah, but somebody might want to talk to me."** **If they want to talk to you that badly, they'll leave you a message. They'll send you an email**. And here's the thing on emails: you don't have to answer instantly. You don't even have to have it on all day. I typically turn off my emails for hours on end, then tackle things in one fell swoop, and then get back to work. But, we've become accustomed to email being an instant communication. We've become accustomed to having an almost instant reply when we send someone an email. Don't fall into that trap. **It's your inbox, not theirs**. And, if it's that important, I promise you they will phone.

So, just remember, **emails are not time sensitive typically**. But people do want a response. Many of my clients realize that sometimes it takes me as many as 48 hours to reply to an email, especially if they want me to do stuff. That's the way I work and, to be honest, most of my clients tend to follow that. If it's an email, I promise it's not urgent. Urgent stuff warrants a phone call.
Get some help!

So, coming back to your working habits, get into a routine of getting some work done. But, **if it genuinely is too much, then you need to think about perhaps offloading some of this work to subcontractors**.

Now, there's a whole load of things you can dish out to other people. First and foremost, and this is something that I've learned particularly well, is that you can **offload your bookkeeping**. There are plenty of people out there who will do your bookkeeping for not a lot of money per hour and probably less than you can earn in that hour, so it's going to be a good investment. Dish out your bookkeeping.

What else can you get other people to do? Are there certain elements of your work that you can delegate or outsource to other people?

I have a graphic designer. She works for me and it works incredibly well. She works for me on a project-by-project basis. I pay her a fixed fee. The work gets done to a very good standard. She understands the way I work and it works well. She earns a little bit of money. I get the client stuff done. Yes, I'm giving away a little bit of my profit, but the work gets done and, more importantly, I don't have to do it. She's far more efficient at graphic design and image manipulation than I am, so why shouldn't I pay her? It probably takes her an hour for something that would take me two or three, maybe four hours because she's far more experienced and efficient with that kind of work.

> "Only focus on stuff that only you can do. The rest of it can (and should) be contracted out!"

I have programmers who work for me on a project basis. Why? Because they're far better at coding than I am, far more efficient. So, again, what would take me three hours-ish might take them just 45 minutes. It just means that I can get more done with the time I have available.

The ultimate goal of contracting stuff out is to enable you to focus more on the stuff that you're best at. This could be sales, it could be working with clients, it could be product delivery or fulfilment. Whatever your core strength is, try and work out a way to contract out the other stuff to free up your own productivity.

The Tim Ferriss book, *The 4-Hour Workweek*, revolves around this philosophy of subcontracting work out, giving it to people who are far more efficient than you while maintaining the client relationship and making sure that you've got a profit in between. Yes, in his case, he's taken it to an extreme where he earns quite a lot of money, farms almost all of it out, and just keeps a healthy margin. There's nothing wrong with that. Arguably, that's where most people should be aiming in their business.

As your business grows, you'll possibly **employ people to do stuff**, which means that you're again delegating stuff to others so you can maximize your time doing what you do best.

So, an important question to ask yourself on all of your work, not just some of it, all of your work, "Is there something here that I can delegate out to somebody else and still maintain control?"

Now, I know that when we're self-employed we're very precious about what we do and we like to feel that sense of pride about getting paid for doing a good job. But, to be honest, as long as the work is done well and is delivered on time, clients don't really mind who did it.

So, I would say don't be precious about your work and don't think that you have to have your name attached to everything that happens in your business. You don't have to be superman or superwoman, you just have to be good at making sure that the work gets done. **Getting help is NOT a sign of weakness** - it usually reflects the fact that your

> "You'll never be successful if you try and do everything yourself!"

business is growing and you can't do everything yourself!

Of course you're still ultimately responsible for the work - after all, it's your business - but for the most part, my clients don't care whether it's me who does the programming or whether it's done by somebody based in another city or even another country. In fact, much of this book has been dictated and recorded and transcribed because I'm not an efficient typist. So, it's more effective and efficient, a good use of time for me, to dictate what I want to write and have it transcribed by somebody else. I can dictate at over 100 words a minute. I can't type that fast for sure.

So, have a think about **what else you can do to reduce your own workload**. You could delegate out some of your marketing. You could delegate the task of answering your phone. Virtual assistants or virtual PAs are very popular these days, especially with small businesses. This is particularly good if you spend a lot of time with clients and you're unable to answer the phone yourself. It means that you'll never miss a call and also that sales calls can be screened and not waste your time.

I seriously suggest you try hiring in some help. It could well be that you contract out somebody to manage your CRM system or your email marketing system. Once you start thinking about it, you realize that there's absolutely loads of stuff in your business that other people can do. You really don't have to do it all. So if you have the profits and the turnover and it will save you time and money, I'd suggest that you get as much help as you need.

What if that's still not enough?

Thinking about your workload, here's a question you need to consider: If you're working flat out selling as much as you possibly can and still not making much of a profit, then something in your business has to change.

One option is to **increase your turnover with less profit per job by contracting out more of the work**. That's fine. High volume with low margin can be a great business model. Or, **it could well be that you need to put your prices up**. I discuss when it's a good idea and a good time to increase your fees in detail in Chapter 19.

But it could also mean that your whole business model is wrong, in which case you need to have a proper think about what you're doing and how you're doing it. You can then decide whether you need to do things differently. You might decide to sell different goods or services, branch out a bit, or change your target customers. Either way, if you really can't cope, you might end up having to make some fundamental changes in your business.

" If you're selling all that you can, working flat out but still not making any money then, something has to change!"

So, I hope that's given you some ideas on how you can maximize your time because, ultimately, time is all we have. There is no shortage of money in the world, even if you don't have as much as you'd like. The mission for anybody in business is to attract some of that money and to try and make sure that you're earning it on a consistent basis. That's your mission.

A key thing to remember is that **nobody builds a successful business all on their own**.

Because, ultimately, the finite resource, the only finite resource we have in our lives and in our business is time. How you use that time is critical. Even if that means you need to invest in some personal coaching, go on a time management course, invest in some software to help you organize yourself or join a business group for mutual support and motivation, then do it. If it means you get more stuff done and ultimately you can develop a more successful business, do it.

Please, whatever you do, get organized. Use your time effectively and hire some help if you need it. Don't be precious about your work.

Smashing Unemployment

Chapter 8
Do What You Say And Build A Great Reputation

Having a great reputation among cust mers and other businesses is very important. You want to be known as somebody who sells good products and services, but is also reliable and consistent.

This might not sound particular important or exciting - after all who ever won an award for just turning up on time? But it's all part of growing a successful business.

Over my years in business I've met a good few thousand people at networking and business events. These are great opportunities to make good contacts and find potential customers. But if you want to impress people, you need to make a point of following up on contacts and following through with what you promise.

Unfortunately a lot of people miss opportunities because they simply don't bother to do what they say they were going to. And you'll hear a whole range of excuses such as: "Well, you know, I haven't had time. I was too busy. Something came up. I had to do my hair. The car needed washing. The dog was sick" and all of this stuff. There's a million different reasons why it didn't happen.

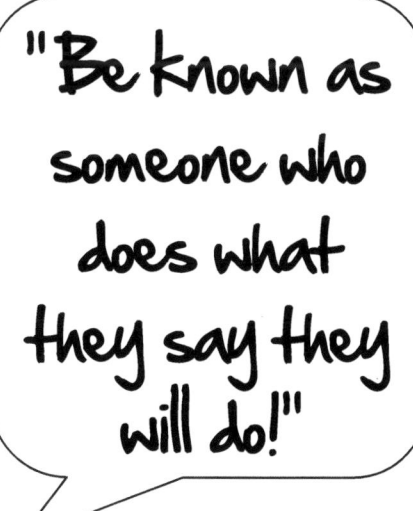

"Be known as someone who does what they say they will do!"

But in my experience, if you're committed to business growth, you don't just talk about what you say you're going to do. You go ahead and do it. **Success is for those who go and do what's required to build a business**. It's not always fun. It ain't always sexy. Sometimes, it's just plain dull and uninteresting. But, the essential thing is that you need to go and do it.

There's a good recent example. I was at a networking event and I met a woman who had not long started her event management company. I do a lot of networking and I know a lot of people who also do a lot of networking. She told me that she wanted to get out into more networking groups. I said, "I'll tell you what. Here's my card. Send me a quick email tomorrow to remind me and I'll send you a list of the networking groups that I think you could get into quickly and easily." Six months later, I was still waiting for the email. I gave her an easy opportunity to find out more information that might help her business. All she had to do was follow it up.

The biggest travesty is that there are plenty of people in business who are just like that. What they say they will do (and what they say they want) don't match up with their actions. If you want to develop a good reputation in your marketplace and with your clients, simply do what you say you're going to do. If you say you're going to send someone an email, make sure that you do it. If you're slightly delayed, apologize for the delay, but make sure that you do it. If you're going to follow up with something, make sure you do it. If you're going to do this at a business event, make sure that you make a note on a business card, or on a Post-it note, or put it in your phone. But, do it. Because, sadly, far too few people do.

But here's another example: Every year at the exhibitor training session for an annual business event here in Leicestershire I tell people to follow up with everything. Even if they're not your target market, follow up. At the event, I hand out loads of cards to almost all exhibitors so that they can contact me to discuss possible business opportunities. Guess how many follow up? Fewer than 1 in 20.

Now, it doesn't necessarily mean that I'm going to be a particularly good client for any of them. In some cases, I won't ever buy from them because they don't offer something I could use. But, that doesn't mean I don't know someone who might be a good customer. Again, it's what people say they will and what they will actually do don't match up. You can't build a successful business being like that.

> "You only have to be consistently good at customer service to stand out from your competition!"

Even if it's something as simple as saying, "I'll tell you what. Let's go for a coffee next week. I'll send you an email." If I don't send you the email, you're not going to be going for a coffee, but what's that done to your credibility? You've just shot yourself down in flames if that's you. Do what you say you're going to do.

Now, don't get me wrong, I'm not perfect on this. I sometimes get this wrong. Goodness knows how many times I said I would do something and I didn't. But, I'm far more conscious now of the fact that my reputation depends on the simple fact that I turn up when I say I will or do what I say I'm going to. Once word gets around that you're reliable and get stuff done, success happens so much more quickly simply because you are known as dependable.

In the U.K., we regularly hear stories about poor customer service. But here's the thing. You don't have to be outstanding at customer service to get a great reputation. You just have to be consistently good. Not brilliant, not amazing, you don't have to wow your customers, you just have to be consistently good. Do what you say you're going to do and develop a reputation for being that way. In all honesty, that's just common decency. All we want as human beings is straightforward, honest, trustworthy behaviour. But, sadly, it's lacking. Don't be that kind of person and don't allow your business to become known as unreliable or untrustworthy.

Chapter 9
Getting Your Marketing Right

In this Chapter, we're going to discuss the very important subject of marketing. I'll talk about sales in the next chapter, but marketing comes first, because that's how you find your potential customers. Selling is what you do once you've identified the customers.

Marketing is one of the most misunderstood elements of any business, especially within the small businesses and self-employed community. But it really doesn't need to be all that complex. It can certainly be made an awful lot easier if you get to grips with 3 very simple, but very logical, concepts; knowing your market; i.e. your ideal customer; sending the right message and using the most appropriate forms of media for your business.

What is marketing?

But what exactly is marketing? A lot of people see marketing as advertising, and promotion, and getting your brand out there, and telling people about what you do. That is certainly part of it. But I once heard a very succinct of the subject - **that marketing is simply the methods that you use to get and to keep customers**.

"Marketing is simply the things you do to get and keep customers!"

Now, methods, you might think, well, that's all about the promotions or about the advertising. But, it goes a little bit deeper than that and I'm going to cover some things now which are absolutely vital to your success in marketing. If you get these right, I promise you that you will outperform your competition in the marketing game almost without exception because 90% of people in small businesses these days get their marketing completely and totally wrong.

So, think about this, we're going to look at getting and keeping customers. **Marketing doesn't stop when you get a customer**. Marketing starts when you get a customer because you've got to keep that customer. You have to nurture that customer. You have to keep them happy. You have to give them great customer service. You have to give them a price and an agreement that's acceptable to them. All of that is within your marketing because it's great having the best sales technique and marketing technique in the world but if, when they become a customer, they have a bad experience, then they're going to want to run from you. And not only that, they will tell all of their friends as well. *So, the key is to try and get this whole process right*.

Knowing your market

So, here we go, the first concept: **your marketing starts with knowing your market**. It doesn't start with a website. It doesn't start with advertising. It doesn't start with business cards. It doesn't start with leaflets and flyers. It starts with knowing your market.

> "Marketing always starts with your MARKET. In other words; the people you're trying to sell to!"

Now, what do I mean by this? If you've been in business a little while or you've read a little bit about business, you'll know that a lot of folks go on about knowing your ideal customer. Who is you're ideal customer? Now, this may sound daft and for years I ignored it, but this is an absolutely vital question to answer.

The reason is that if you don't know your customers or your ideal or typical customers, **then you're going to waste as much as 80% of your marketing time, effort, and money trying to promote to the wrong people**. That's right. As much as 80% of marketing is wasted by small businesses because they don't fully understand or even know their customers. They haven't done any market research at all; or they haven't done the right sort of marketing or not enough.

Now, that doesn't mean you should spend an awful lot of time or money asking questions or doing surveys just to see what people think. You can actually do this quite quickly and easily: **just talk to those people you'd like to do business with**. Even if they have no intention of doing business with you, you can find out a lot about what they think, what they buy, and why they buy it just by talking to them. Even better, if you tell them that you'll buy them lunch for example or just have a chat with them, you can make notes, and learn a lot from this.

The key here is that **it will give you a demographic of your ideal customer**. And that demographic is who they are, where they live, what they buy, why they buy it, how much they might spend, what they like, how old they are, what kind of car they drive, how much money they earn, where they shop, what gender they are, what age they are, what race they are, what kind of things they're into, what kind of interests they have, what do they like to do in their hobbies, etc.

All this information is important simply because, **once you get inside the mind of your potential customer, selling to them becomes an awful lot easier**, and I'll tell you why shortly.

And you might be surprised at the results. Suppose you sell

ladies' lingerie. You probably assume that there's no point advertising in places predominantly frequented by men. For example, you'd assume that there would be no point in buying a billboard at the local football club because only a small number of women are going to see it. However a lot of men buy lingerie as presents so advertising at a football club could actually bring in business.

What about putting an ad in a business magazine? Well the same logic applies - the overwhelming majority of people in business are men so seeing an advert for lingerie when reading a "business" magazine may be a good way of finding out about your products. However, you need ask yourself whether many people will be inspired to buy lingerie after seeing it in a business magazine.

And once you know your customer, then you've got the opportunity to think about what kind of things you can do to attract them.

What to say to potential customers: your message

That brings me onto the next step which is all about your **message**, what you say to your customers.

"The 2nd part is your MESSAGE. This is all about what you're saying to your MARKET!"

What are you going to say to these customers? Because, once you understand them, talking to them should be fairly straightforward because you'll know them. You will know their language. You will know their concerns. You will know their desires. You will know what they want or what they don't want, what they like and what they don't like, what interests they have and what sparks them.

The great thing about knowing this information about your market is that it makes creating your message so much easier because you're communicating with a particular section of the market who will have a certain language, who will have certain interests.

But, you can't work out this message **until you understand your ideal customer and why they'd be interested in buying your product**.

It would be like me trying to sell cars without understanding anything about why people buy cars. It would make no sense. I'm not a car expert, so I wouldn't even be able to speak the language of those people who are interested in buying cars. In fact, from my point of view, if a car works, that's great. If it doesn't, I phone someone who does know about cars to get some help. That's how little I know about cars. I would never be a great car salesman without doing a lot of research for getting into selling cars. I wouldn't know the messages. I wouldn't know the communications or language that people want to hear when buying cars. I don't even know the demographic of those who buy cars. I simply don't know this stuff, so I'd have to do a lot of research to get to know the market.

Again, if you're an accountant, if you understand your market, you can communicate with them. You can communicate with businesses. You can communicate with individuals who may need a tax return done. But, the message always stems from knowing your market.

Now, the thing with the message, and there's three important elements of it, is that when you're trying to get this across, you've got to pick on three and a half things. (Don't worry, I'll explain the half).
- The first thing is, you need to **tell them who you are.**
- Second, you need to tell people what it is or **what it's about**?
- Finally, you've definitely got to get across to them **"what's in it for me?"**

Now, it used to be, if you read the Yellow Pages, you'd see adverts for say plumbers. It would say, "ABC Plumbers. We do this, this, this, and this. Here's our phone number." And that seemed to be it. This is called 'name, rank, and serial number' marketing. This is who we are, this is what we do, and here's our number, give us a call or whatever. In fact, a lot of times, they didn't have the "give us a call" bit, they just had their number on it and they expected the phone to ring.

These days, that kind of advertising simply doesn't work and you've got to be a little bit smarter than that. Consumers and people in business are a bit smarter than that. They make more complex decisions and you need to adapt to that.

So, what you need in your marketing message is the 3 things: who we are, what we do, and why what we do is good for you as a potential customer. **It's that's "what's in it for me?" as a potential customer that's vital, and that's what 90% of nearly all marketing leaves out.** Why is what we do good for you? What's in it for me as a customer?

Like I said, if you know your market, your messaging becomes so much clearer and sometimes even obvious. So, think about that, who we are, what we do, and why what we do is good for you as a potential customer.

The half bit is a **call to action**. On all marketing, you should have some kind of call-to-action.

What does this mean? Well a call to action is simply an invitation for people to do something.

How many times do you go to a business event and you pick up a business card, and it just goes, "John Smith, Accountant. We do all sorts of accounts. Here's the phone number. Here's our email." That's great, but what's in it for me? What do I do next? Is there a reason I should get in touch with you? Are you any better than my existing accountant. Is there something you're going to do for me which is going to make it worth my while to get in touch at least?

So, can you think of a call to action which stimulates some kind of response?
Now, typically on a website, I encourage our clients to have some kind of giveaway, a free report, a free training course, a free something in exchange for certain information. Then, that starts off a dialogue of marketing messages.

On my business cards, I have "Download a Free Report" from my website. It gets people to my website and I know that only people who are interested in what I have to offer will ever download it, (or my competition trying to spy on me).

The key is, even on a business card, you can have some kind of call to action. Don't just tell who you are, **tell people why what you do is good for them**. Then, the next step is to tell them what to do next to keep the dialogue going.

If you get those 3 and a half things right, I promise you that you will outperform your competition in almost all cases. I'm saying 90% here, and I mean 90% because, as I said earlier, nearly all small businesses get this completely and totally wrong. They go for the name, rank, and serial number type of advertising and marketing and it doesn't work nearly as well as it did. Competition is much more fierce. People's time is more valuable. *You need a darn good reason for your target customer to respond to your message*.
How to deliver your message: using media

The final element of it is **media**. We've covered finding our market, we've covered the messaging, now we're looking at the media. **Media is simply the means and methods by which you get your message across.**

This is what used to be called advertising or promotion. The media is absolutely essential here again, just like the other two, but they follow on from the other two. Most people get this the wrong way round. They'll start with a website without fully understanding their market. They'll get business cards without knowing what kind of message to put on it. And it's wrong. You need to work out the market, message, and media -- in that order.

There are hundreds of potential media (channels) to get your message across. You've got a website, you've got all kinds of social media, you've got all kinds places you can put your company name, your logo, your branding, etc. There are hundreds.

From my point of view, when we work with clients and we build them a website,

> "The 3rd part is MEDIA. This is simply the methods you use to get your MESSAGE in front of your MARKET!"

we get them to think a little bit more well-rounded or holistically about their marketing because it needs to be coherent. Their messaging needs to be coherent and their media needs to be coherent.

Your website is a marketing channel. Social media "platforms", including Twitter, Facebook, LinkedIn, Pinterest, whichever, all of these social media channels are also marketing channels or media.
Any sort of advertising uses a media to deliver the message. Putting a billboard over a football club, again it's a media. Putting an ad in the newspaper, it's a media. Sending out

letters to potential customers, it's media. Your business card is a media. Your leaflet is a media.

The point I'm making here is that using the right media for your business is just as important as knowing your customer and sending the right message. It's just as important as identifying potential customers and telling them who you are we, what you do, why it's good for them and what you'd like them to do next. And it will be even more powerful if you make your message in the "language" of the potential customer because it shows that you understand your ideal customer.

A lot of businesses get use the "scattergun" approach by trying to cover lots of different media. But you'll be a lot more successful (and save time and money) if you **pick the channels appropriate to your market**. For example, if you're selling to consumers online, spending a lot of time on LinkedIn won't be nearly as productive as spending that time on Twitter and Facebook. Why? Because your market for consumer products probably isn't on LinkedIn.

The same thing applies to Facebook if you're selling business-to-business. People don't go to Facebook to hire an accountant. They go to look at what their friends are up to and to share what they've been up to. So, if you're an accountant, from a social media perspective, Facebook is going to be largely a waste of time. I'm not saying there aren't ways of getting around that if you pay for advertising, but for the most part, using it as a free channel is a waste.

> "Always use MEDIA (channels) appropriate to your MARKET. Put your MESSAGE where your potential clients are!"

However, if you're an accountant, LinkedIn is the place to go. If you sell lingerie, LinkedIn is not the place to go because people typically don't go onto LinkedIn to buy underwear!

So, **choose your channels appropriately according to where your market is**. If you sell to women, being a sponsor of your local golf club is probably not going to be the most effective channel. I'm not saying that women don't play golf, but most golfers tend to be men. However, more women play tennis as a proportion of the tennis-playing demographic so advertising to women might be a better fit there. So, **if your target customers are men** and they are golfers or a demographic that is interested in golf, then a golf club sponsorship or golf club advertising might work for you.

If you sell to consumers, going to business networking events really isn't going to be the hottest thing for you. Why? Because people go to business networking events to make contacts and look for business opportunities with other businesses. Going to a County Show might be more effective in this case. However **if you sell to small businesses**, for example, going to a business networking group is a bit like a buffet of potential clients.

One particularly interesting demographic is **older people**. Email marketing is probably not going to be the most efficient channel. Why? Because a large proportion of elderly people don't use the internet. They didn't grow up with email like the rest of us and, for some, email is terrifying.

Interestingly though, the fastest growing demographic on Facebook at the moment is the over-50's, the Silver Surfers. But for the most part, the older generation will respond to more traditional marketing; send them a catalogue by post, use door to door leaflets or an advert on TV or local radio.

On the other hand, if you're selling to **young, dynamic people**, you will probably want to be on the latest, most-popular social media. You will probably want to be on the forefront of the electronic media. Mobile phone advertising might be a great methodology for you or text messaging marketing.

Pulling it all together

Now, I hope you're getting a picture here. The picture is that you should go where your customers are. You should speak the language that your customers speak. And you should know what your customers are interested in. So, hopefully, you've got that.

Always, always, always make sure you know where your customers are coming from.

Always make sure that you **know why they buy from you**. Track the results of your marketing to understand what it was that they responded to in your marketing and then ask why they responded that way. With this information you can refine your target marketing and increase sales by making your marketing strategy even more effective.

And, finally, you should always **aim at having between six and ten active marketing channels**, or media, on the go at any one time. That sounds a lot but remember that includes each different social media platforms; Twitter, Facebook, LinkedIn, and Pinterest. There's 4 to start with. Your website, blogging, email marketing add another 3 channels. And don't forget more traditional types of marketing, such as attending networking events or exhibiting at a local trade show.

Choose your media according to your market. As I said at the beginning of this chapter, if you get this wrong you're going to be wasting more than 80% of your marketing time and money, and I don't want that for anyone. I would like your marketing to be effective, aimed at the right people with the right message in the right way. That's what all of your marketing should be.

And if you want your marketing to be successful, then you can learn from some of the most successful entrepreneurs.

Charles Schwab started one of the biggest and most successful investment companies on Wall Street back in 1975. One of his best-known phrases is, *"80% of my marketing is wasted. The problem is that I don't know which 80%."*

> "Always make sure you know where your clients are coming from. You want to maximise the marketing that works!"

In your business, you should always know which of your marketing channels is working, which of your marketing efforts is producing the best results.

You should never be in the position where you don't know where your customers are coming from because it could well be that one of your marketing channels is outperforming the others by 5:1 and, if you know that, you can put more effort and emphasis onto it to maximize those results.

So, there's lots you can do. But, have as many as you can physically possibly handle and, remember to track the results.

I know I've covered a lot of ground in this section and there are hundreds, if not thousands, of marketing books out there that you could potentially buy if you want to develop a more sophisticated marketing strategy. But for now, keep your marketing simple. The simpler your marketing, the easier it will be to manage and more likely to attract new customers and keep existing customers.

Chapter 10
How to Make Sales Work for You

In this chapter, we're going to tackle one of the most difficult and grossly misunderstood parts of running a business, and that's selling.

No matter what business you're in, whether that's selling perfumes at a market stall, whether it's selling electronics online, whether that's selling websites (as I do), or selling legal services, at some point you are going to have to do some kind of selling. You are going to have to engage with potential customers and you are going to have to try and take them by the hand and lead them to the point where they part with some money.

If you think that you're ever going to escape this process in your business, then you are very much mistaken. Nobody gets out of this. *No business, unless you're a defence contractor for the government, gets out of having to sell and, to some extent, even defence contractors have to sell themselves.*

With that in mind, let's try and put together something which can help you make sense of selling and then help you become far more effective at selling than almost everybody else in your field. I don't say that lightly because I understand how badly most businesses - and by that I mean over

"The follow-up process accounts for around 80% of all sales!"

75% - of businesses don't sell effectively and, as a result, don't get the results that they could.

So, what can we do to change that? Well, let's think about a couple of statistics. Just under 50% of professional salespeople don't follow up properly. That's just under 50% of people who get paid to sell. They don't follow up properly. However, the follow up process accounts for around 80% of all successful sales. You might have noticed a bit of a theme here. The common denominator there is the **follow-up**.

But, it's important to take a step back for a moment because I want to introduce you to the **concept of process**. Successful businesses have processes. This means that they don't have to reinvent the wheel with every customer. And for you to be successful you need to have some kind of process. Otherwise, you'll be constantly stressed keeping up with where you are in the sales process, how it's going, what they're saying, who said what to whom, what needs to be done, what's left to be done, what the client's expectations are, and so on.

It's an absolute nightmare if you don't have processes. And sales is one of those situations where **processes can make the difference between success and struggle**. I'm not saying that glibly, it's an absolute fact. As soon as we started introducing proper processes into our sales and in our business for our web design company, our profits went up, our sales went up, our ability to manage the work went up, and to be honest, our work/life balance improved as well.

So, how do we develop our own sales process?

One of the easiest things to do is to take some time out and write a customer process or journey. So when somebody first enquires about what it is you do, or you pick up a lead, you know what to do next, by following your sales process.

Then, when you've done that next thing, what's after that?

For example, in my web design business, when I pick up a lead, I generally try and **make an appointment** to go and have a chat with the person or the business owners. I have a **checklist of questions** that I want answered during that process and I talk to them and I tell them that I have a checklist because I want to fully understand what they're aiming at and what they feel that their website needs to do.

The next step of the process is for me to go away and **complete a proposal**. Now, this is a template-based proposal, so I don't have to write it unique every time. I just include bits that are pertinent to the discussion that I had with the potential client, based on my notes and the questions that they answered. Then, I send that over to them.

I **follow up with a phone call** to make sure that they got the proposal and whether they had a chance to take a look at it. That, typically is within 24 hours. If I sent it on a Tuesday, I'll phone them on Wednesday. I don't expect them to have read it, I just want to make sure that's it's arrived that I'm waiting for them to read it. A couple of days later, **I'll follow up again to see if they've had a chance to read it** and to answer any questions. **At that point, we start the actual negotiation, dealing with their queries and overcoming any objections**.

In our business, there aren't many objections about price because price related issues are usually sorted out by our money-back guarantee and payment plan. Usually it's a question of how they can fit it in or whether they want it at all. From there, we have a follow-up process, a combination of emails and phone calls literally until they buy or tell us, "No, this isn't for us."

Unless and until they've told us a definite 'no' then they stay in the sales process with regular calls and emails. However, **if I've not had a definitive answer after a few weeks I'll usually ask them if they're likely to buy a website from us any point soon**. I simply use the excuse that we need to adjust their status on our database for now. Most of the time people make a decision at that point. Even if the answer is no then at least we'll not be following-up for ages and wasting precious time.

Now, that is a very straightforward and simple process for selling. To be honest, we didn't invent it. I picked it up from somewhere else. So feel free to adapt and deploy.

> "Having a sales system always brings increased sales because fewer leads are overlooked!"

Having said all of that we also have a process that goes beyond the sale because, **the real work starts AFTER you've made THE sale**. But, we know that following our sales process works. I'd strongly recommend that you devise your own sales process and implement it.

One of the key things for this process is to think about what you do and when, and literally write it down. Write yourself a checklist and, every time you develop a lead, put it into that checklist. It could be a chart on a board and you plot where people are on that chart. It could list: sales development proposal, first follow-up, appointment, follow-up calls, whatever it needs. There's a process here. If you stick to that process and refine it as you're going along your sales success rates will improve. And if there's things that need improving invest the time and effort to change it and improve it. It should always be a case of constant improvement.

Why people won't buy

The next thing is you have a look at the objectives that people can come up with as to why they wouldn't buy and try and think of reasons how you can overcome them. Normally, when people object in some way, shape, or form, it's because of one (or more) of the following:

- you haven't explained things to them fully or
- you haven't shown them the benefits of what you do over the cost of the thing; or
- they genuinely can't afford it or
- they're just wasting your time, and I mean wasting your time. There's a lot of time wasters out there, especially in the work that I do.

And remember: follow up is the key. As I said earlier, over 75% of sales are often left on the table because people don't follow up properly. Usually, people won't buy after the first or second follow up. Sometimes, it can be as many as six or seven follow ups. But, if you give up after five, and the next call or the next email was the one that could have turned them into a customer, you've shot yourself in the foot instantly and your success is hampered.

"Follow up". I can't emphasize this enough. Follow up until they buy, die, or tell you to get lost. It's really that simple. And, even if they do tell you to get lost, keep in touch. They may not become a customer now, but if they've had a good experience during the sales and follow-up process, they may become a customer at some other point or they may know somebody who has an urgent need for what you're offering. So, don't get frustrated by this. Follow up.

"80% of sales are made afer the 5th follow-up. Just make sure you hang in there!"

Overall, developing leads is down to your marketing and your marketing should always be response based, as I discussed in the chapter 'Getting Your Marketing Right'.

When you get to an appointment, the key is listening. You're there offering a service. They're there interested in whatever it is you're offering so listen to what they have to say. If they have concerns, you need to think about how you can address those concerns. Is there a problem that you can solve here? **That's often what selling is all about. It's problem solving.** How can you make their lives better? How can you enhance their situation? How can you make their lives easier? How can you make them more money? How can you save them money?

There's a whole load of reasons why people buy. This appointment and this fact gathering is all about that particular information. What is it that they're after you to fix? So, listen. Make notes. As we do in our web design business, is there a series of questions that you can answer to get at the heart of the matter?

Then, **put them into your follow-up process.** This starts when you send them a proposal and follow up within 24 hours just to make sure they got it. You're not asking for a decision about the job, you just want to make sure they got it. It lets them know you're on the case.

But, it also gives you the opportunity to make an appointment to follow up again. You could say something like: "Okay. That's brilliant. I know you've just received the proposal, Mr. Potential Customer. I'm going to leave you with it for a few days. Is it okay if I give you a call on Tuesday next week, sometime late morning?" Very rarely will they say no unless they have an appointment, in which case, you reschedule it again and you put that follow up in your diary. When you hang up, send them a quick email saying, "Looking forward to having a chat with you on Tuesday next week late morning or eleven-ish." It lets them know that, again, you're on the case. This is what's known as professional selling, and you keep doing this until you get a decision -- yes, no, or get lost.

Most people give up way too soon. I'm talking about 80% of people, especially in small businesses, give up way too soon.

Getting round the stalling tactics

A lot of people, especially here in Britain, are not terribly decisive. Instead of saying no to you, they say, "Well, I need to think about it." Or, "I need to talk to my accountant." Or, "I have to discuss it with my business partners." Or, "I'm not sure." Or, "Can you give me a call?" Or, "No. We're not going to do this for now." The hardest part of the following up is trying to get through the BS to understand what it is they're trying to tell you.

If they're stalling and if you feel that they're stalling, they either find it difficult to say no, (which is very common), or they're just stalling for time and they've genuinely got a reason for doing so.

But, again, try and ask some questions and try and get to this. I've simply asked customers, "Is there any particular reason why you wouldn't want to go with us now? What is it that seems to be getting in the way?" Usually, if they're stalling, you'll get a very vague and woolly, unspecific answer. I've had things like, "Oh, we're really busy in our business right now. We've got some things to sort out." Sometimes they'll say, "We don't have the cash flow." Sometimes they'll say, "Well, we've not had time to discuss it in great detail and we'll come back to you." All of that is just stalling tactic. So, again, make an appointment to follow up. Do it and follow up, and follow up.

This doesn't mean that you're calling them every other day, but it does mean that you're maintaining a modicum of control in the situation. If they don't want to make a decision and they don't want to say "No," then that's up to them.

I had a lead with a law firm not long ago and I went to see the guy. We had a discussion and we batted it back and forwards. He asked me some questions on an email and I sent him responses on an email. Then, I phoned him up and I kept leaving voicemails. I kept emailing him. After something around a dozen attempts to follow up (over a period of about 10 weeks), I simply sent him an email, "I'm going to take you off the CRM system as a potential customer. If you're interested in what we have, please come back to us and we can discuss it further". I did this because I had to make the decision as to whether this was going to be worth all the follow up because it does take time and, sometimes, you do have to make that decision.

But don't give up too soon! Don't give up on the third or fourth follow up. You need to get to ten in my opinion. Get to ten follow-ups, a combination of email and phone call. If they haven't responded by then, move on. But keep in touch. Add them to your database, or your email list, and keep in touch. It could well be genuinely that they are stacked out with work and don't have time to deal with it. But, whatever you do, just don't fall off their radar. You should be sending information out to your list of potential and past customers anyway. That's all part of your ongoing marketing strategy. The key is to follow up. Follow up, follow up, follow up. **80% of success in sales is in the follow up**.

Asking for the sale

So, what do you do on these follow ups? Well, the first time you follow up, you effectively say -- you're going to have to at some point say, "Look, is there any reason why you won't go ahead with this?" Or, "Okay, do you want to do it?" Or, "Do you want to place your order?" Or, at some point, you are going to have to say, "Do you want to go for it?" It's called "asking for the sale." To be honest, it's possibly the most difficult thing to do because how do you phrase it without coming across as aggressive? But, all you're doing is saying something like, "Is there any reason why we couldn't get the ball rolling now?" "Do you want to get the ball rolling?" I know it sounds easy but it can be quite terrifying when you're in front of a potential customer or when you're on the phone to a potential customer.

> "You need to get good at asking for the sale. Your success depends on it!"

Sometimes, even I struggle with this. But, ultimately, you've got to say, "Great. You like what we're offering, do you want to go for it?" It's at that point where indecisive people will start to balk. If they're unconvinced about your proposal, they'll start to make excuses. Or, if they genuinely don't know whether they can make a decision, will put it off.

It's up to you to maintain the initiative and then put them into your follow-up process. And you need to get good at asking for the order. There's nothing wrong with asking for the order and you need to accept that you're not going to win every sale that you attempt to get. It's just the nature of the game.

Michael Jordan (possibly the most famous basketball player ever) didn't score every hoop that he shot at. It's as simple as that. But, if he's 70% successful when it mattered, that is a massive success ratio. But, if you don't take the shots, then you'll never win. That's a good principle to remember. **You lose 100% of the sales you don't follow up with**. So get good at asking for the order.

Making that first phone call

Some people are genuinely terrified at the prospect of making calls, picking up the phone to ask for business. Often, in the first instance, it's a question of "We had a chat at this networking event, Mr. Potential Customer, and you were vaguely interested. Would you like to get together for a cup of coffee and we can talk about it?" Notice that I didn't try selling him anything. I didn't say, "Let's go and make a deal." I simply said, "You expressed an interest in what we're up to. Can I come over and have a chat? I'll even bring the coffee, the sugar, the milk, and some hot water if that's what you want."

All you're doing at this stage is asking for an appointment. That first call is asking for the appointment. You're not trying to make a sale. You're not trying to convince them of anything. You're just simply saying, "Let's have a chat. I'll be there no longer than 20 minutes if that's okay with you because I know you're busy and just get together and kick it over."

Then you go over with your series of questions. You listen, ask your questions, and see whether there's some way you can work together.

An important thing to bear in mind is that, at some point, you'll be asked a question you don't know the answer to. Chances are good that you'll get an awkward lead. But don't panic because this will only be once in a while and the key thing is to just do it. Take it as a learning experience and you might just make a sale anyway.

> "Getting good at sales takes practice. So hang in there!"

A good thing to remember is that **Selling takes practice**. If you're new to selling, it can be very terrifying. And, if you're really that terrified, you can always farm out the selling process to a sales fulfilment company. There are plenty of people out there who will pick up the phone for you and they'll have a much better chance of closing the deal because they are experts in tele-sales.

Obviously, you'll pay them for it which will reduce your profit. Either way, if you're genuinely terrified at the idea of making phone calls to arrange a meeting or discuss a proposal, find a way to get over it. A very good friend of mine went to hypnosis to overcome his fear of selling and it worked. It may seem a little unconventional, but he was literally shivering at the prospect of picking up the phone.

So, work out a route that's going to be okay for you. Work out a method that's going to work for you. And above all, selling takes practice. If you've got a good process, that helps. If you understand the journey from lead to sale, that helps. But, ultimately, you've got to play your part. You're going to have to pick up the phone, you're going to have to write that email and you're going to have to follow up.

Terrifying as it may be, always bear in mind that if you don't sell, you don't eat. It's really that simple in business. If you don't sell, you don't have a business, just a badly paying hobby. In some respects, it's more important to be a sales and marketing expert than an expert in your field because **you can have a mediocre product and, if you can sell it well, you'll do well**. You could have the best product on the planet but, if you can't sell it, you're going to go hungry. It really is that simple.

The success in your business boils down to your ability to market and sell. It's not about how great the product is. History is littered with great products and services that never got off the shelf because they weren't marketed well. Don't be that. Get a good sales process.

The final ingredient: Confidence

Hopefully, I've checked all the boxes and covered pretty much everything you need in your sales process there, but the final point is confidence. Don't be afraid of being wrong. **Don't be afraid of making a mistake**. Nothing will ever go perfectly forever in any business. It doesn't matter who you are, or what business you're in, nothing is going to go perfectly all the time.

> "The success in your business boils down to your ability to market and sell!"

Don't be afraid of making mistakes and don't be afraid of being wrong. And don't be afraid of not winning orders. In our web design business, if we get to the point of having an appointment with the prospective client, we win on average 50% of the sales that we attempt to get. That's an absolutely huge number in selling. You might want to do some research to find out the typical sales success rates in your business sector and start with a more realistic target, especially if this is your first time running your own business.

But **you should never be afraid of rejection**. We're not afraid of people saying no because we realise that, when people go somewhere else for what we offer, that's up to them. The chances are good we weren't going to win them as a customer anyway. Just put the phone down, add them to your email list and move on. Don't cry about it.

When you're in business, and especially when you're self-employed, you have to be able to handle rejection. Handling rejection is one of the hardest things about being self-employed. Potential clients will say no both to what you're offering and how you offer it.

The thing to remember is that **they're not rejecting you, they're rejecting your offering**. It's not personal. In all honesty, most people don't think enough about you to reject you. All they're doing is rejecting what you've pitched at them. Now, if you have an obnoxious personality, possibly there's a bit of objecting to you. But, for the most part, they're only objecting to what you've put in front of them. So, don't be afraid of not winning orders and don't let that dent your confidence.

So, go out there and spend some time developing your sales process. Spend some time looking at objections and how you can overcome them. Spend some time practicing how to ask for the order and following up. Above all, go out there and do it. Don't over think it - just go and do it because, if you don't do it, you'll go hungry.

Chapter 11
Why You Should Hang Around With (and Learn From) the Right People

In this chapter, I'd love to be able to share some things which have been painfully learned for me and also for many of the people I know who have gone on to build successful businesses.

It revolves around understanding the need to hang around with the right people and listen and learn from the right sources.

Now, this is a toughie because, if you've never been in business before and you don't know many people who are in business, you'll typically end up hanging around with a group of other business people, especially if you go networking.

Here's a thought:

Now, if you're a parent—and I don't know whether you are or not—but if you're a parent, you'll know instinctively that you don't want your kids hanging around with kids who swear a lot, whose parents drink a lot, whose parents smoke

"We don't like our kids hanging around with negative people. So why would you do that yourself!"

Up and Running

a lot. You don't want your teenager hanging around with those who drink, swear, do drugs, and get into fights. Why? Because we know that we are influenced by our environment and we know that young people are especially impressionable by those who seem cool, popular, fashionable, and exciting.

As a parent, I know that I don't want my kids hanging around with those who are a bad influence, even though I did that when I was young.

But, the point is this, **influence doesn't stop when you get older**. Your ability to be influenced rarely changes. You become a little bit wiser. You become more stuck in your own viewpoints and arguably less malleable in the way you think, but people are still influenced.

Everyone is influenced

If you don't believe that, then just ask yourself the question as to when you last bought something because it was on a sale and you thought the price was good. Of course, you were being influenced. You were being manipulated into buying something because you thought you were getting a good deal. That's still influence. It still happens.

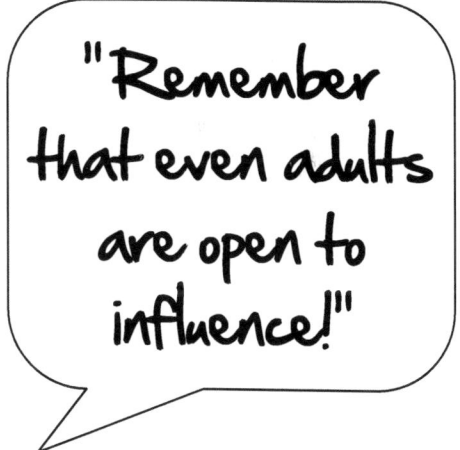
"Remember that even adults are open to influence!"

Marketing people are particularly clever at this. So don't assume that you're not open to influence.

Anyway, let's come back to the point. One of the things that I've learned in being self-employed is that most of the people who are in business are doing okay. I'd say that around 50% of people are getting by, they're doing alright. In my experience, there's around a quarter of people who are experiencing some level of success and out of that quarter there's a few percent who are doing very well indeed. But, that leaves 25 percent-ish of people in business who are only just scraping by.

It's these 'just surviving' people I found to be the most dangerous when you're starting in business or self-employment. You will meet a lot of these people at networking events. They all look great. They've often got very nice clothes. They've got the flashiest business cards. They have the best sales patter. They do the best 60-second speech. But, they are broke. What they say and what they do don't add up.

Unfortunately, and I know I'll take some flack for this, but I've seen plenty of examples of it and, unfortunately, many who go to networking events are in this camp. They'll talk a great talk about how great they are, about how wonderful what they do is, about how it's going to change the world, and a year later they're gone. They're back in employment because they really just couldn't make what they said match up with what they did.

> "Emulate only those who actually walk the talk!"

Don't get me wrong here, people don't succeed for a variety of reasons. But, in my experience, most people who truly want to succeed do so in a variety of different ways, maybe not instantly but they do so eventually.

The key is you've got to try and iron out those people who are not going to be a particularly good influence on you. In my experience, those who are constantly going out for lunch and constantly going out to meetings are often so busy lunching and meeting that they don't actually get any work done or they don't have clients to do any for. I've been there and done that and it's not clever.

There was a time in 2004, when I ran a training business, when I went to ten networking events in one week. It was frightening. I don't know how much money I spent, but that was not typical. I looked back in my diary and I thought, "Oh my God, that's 10 events." Five breakfasts, three lunches, two dinners, guess how much work I did? Zero. Guess how much money I earned from that week? Zero. I was talking a good talk, but actually not walking it.

So, you need to spot these people quickly. I'm not saying you should avoid them completely, but don't let them join your close peer group.

So, having said all of this negative stuff, how can we counter that?

Well, one of the keys to think about is this, be careful of who you listen to. There's an awful lot of cynicism and there's a hell of a lot of critics out there. Interestingly enough, no one ever constructs a statue to honour cynics and critics. Unfortunately, these critics and cynics often tend to be very vocal. And, often, they're only doing it to serve their own fragile ego or to get back at somebody for some perceived slight. **Don't hang around with critics and cynics.** Trust me, they are poison for your business.

"Cynics and critics are poison for you and your business!"

So, who should we hang around with?

First and foremost, you should try and hang around with and learn from those people who are well and truly on their way to where you want to go. People listen to Richard Branson and Bill Gates. Why? Because they achieved massive success and, as a result of it, they've gained some wisdom and this wisdom can be used in your own life and in your own business.

Try and seek out those people who have done what you want to do, who have achieved what you want to achieve. Listen to them, learn from them, and put those lesson into practice if you can.

The key here is implementation. **Go and put what you learn into practice** simply because the good lessons should be taken and used. The bad lessons, once you work out what they are and who they come from, should be ignored.

Also, what you will learn, when you get good and start hanging around with people, is that those who are genuinely willing to help are often those who are well and truly on their way to success.

The great thing about it is this stuff isn't difficult if you're paying attention. But, the crux of it all is this, **not everyone you meet is going to be a good influence**. Not everyone you meet who talks a good game is going to be successful. Those who are bragging about how much money they've got or what kind of car they drive are typically those who are so fearful of failure that they have to justify it all by shouting about how much they've got. Unfortunately, I've found those who are like that tend to be very, very self-centered and are usually not great influences.

Don't get me wrong, I have friends with nice cars, big houses etc, and they're great people, but they've not built a successful business based on bragging. They went and did the stuff that needed to be done to build their business, and those are the kind of people I like hanging around with.

There are loads of sources you can learn from - read books, listen to audio stuff, watch YouTube videos. Learn from those who have been successful and are doing the stuff that you want to do in your business and in your life.

> "Learn from those who've been there and done it!"

But, anyway, the key is this, learn who to hang around with. Hang around those who are definitely going where you want to go or have achieved what you want to achieve and only **listen to the advice of those who have walked the talk**, who are doing and have done what you want to achieve.

Chapter 12
Winning Momentum and Celebrating Success

In this section, I'd like to discuss a couple of important elements that many self-employed people either aren't aware of or may simply overlook. It's all about when your business gets going, you start to get one or two customers coming in and you start to get a little bit of momentum.

I'm a rugby player and referee in my spare time and one of the things that always stands out for me when watching rugby is that, when somebody scores, they always celebrate. They always punch the air and run round the pitch shouting and always make sure that the team feels good. The point is: **they always celebrate**. Whether you watch football, tennis, or rugby, every time a point is scored, they celebrate in some way.

You might wonder why they bother jumping up and down about scoring points but there's actually a psychological reason why they do this, and it's not just because they're paid to do it. The point is that **they want to leverage the good feeling** and that sense of celebration when something good happens.

So let's bring this over into the business world.

It's my belief – and a lot of the business psychologists also agree – that when you get those first few customers, you should celebrate. You should look for a way of celebrating or making yourself feel good about that achievement, even if it's just jumping up and down shouting.

However, I recommend that you do it on your own to begin with; otherwise, your friends and family might think you've lost the plot. But, make sure that you do it as often as you can.

The reason is, when you're self-employed you usually work on your own, and there's often no one around you to celebrate with. There's nobody there to say, "Well done", "Fantastic" or "That's a great job." So, you need to try and manufacture it.

Yes, it can be argued that it's false. But it's part of that "fake it until you make it" approach which can be very powerful. Your subconscious works in one of two ways: it helps to steer you away from danger and painful experiences, but it also helps to steer you towards enjoyable experiences as well. The key thing here is that your subconscious will always do what you've "programmed" it to do. When you physically celebrate a success you're telling your subconscious that you've done really well and that you want to feel this way more often!

The best thing about this though is that those two sides can be leveraged. In this first instance, you're going to try and leverage that good feeling. You want to tell your subconscious very clearly that what we've done here is good because your subconscious can actually go to work behind the scenes to manufacture more of those situations. On the other hand, you want to encourage your brain to process negative experiences - such as losing a sale - in a more productive way, so that you can analyse what went wrong and improve your sales pitch.

Make sure you celebrate successes, however small!

It doesn't really matter how you celebrate but make sure that you do it! I can't emphasize enough how important this is. When we win a new customer, we have a bit of a cheer-fest. It may sound silly and it may go a little bit beyond your comfort zone, but you've already stepped out of the comfort zone enough by being self-employed.

What it does is that it reinforces in your mind that this is a good thing. *Your mind will want to bring more of that into your experience and it will actually help you to move towards doing more of this.* So, celebrate success no matter how small because sometimes all you're going to have is a long series of small successes.

> "Keep doing the things that gave you your initial momentum!"

I would argue that you should be celebrating as much as you possibly can as often as you possibly can. I'm not saying going out drinking because that could become expensive and ultimately damaging. But, in some way, shape, or form, give yourself a psychological or mental pat on the back saying, "That was a good job. Well done. We've done it. We've cracked it. Great stuff." So, celebrate success.

Keep that momentum going!

The next point is maintaining some momentum. A lot of businesses, especially the self-employed, will go out there, to do some networking, send some emails out, put out some flyers, etc. And, as a result, they'll start to get a bit of momentum in their business. As soon as they start getting customers, the marketing effort and momentum-building stops.

Unfortunately, what often happens is that your business can be a bit like a yo-yo where one minute you have loads of work and the next minute you don't have nearly enough because that momentum has been lost. So, it's important to continue doing the things that you started that got the results and gained you that momentum. I'm not saying doing it all day every day, but you need to do it consistently enough and regularly enough and in enough volume to keep it going.

It's a constant juggling act between finding work and doing work

Now, this reminds me of a friend of mine, Adele, who was a web designer in 2001. This was the early days of website design and websites were quite expensive at the time. I was working for an accountancy firm and we needed a website. So, we got Adele in. In getting to know her a little she said that one of her biggest frustrations is that she sells a website, gets paid for it, and then has to go on and find some more income because her income stops.

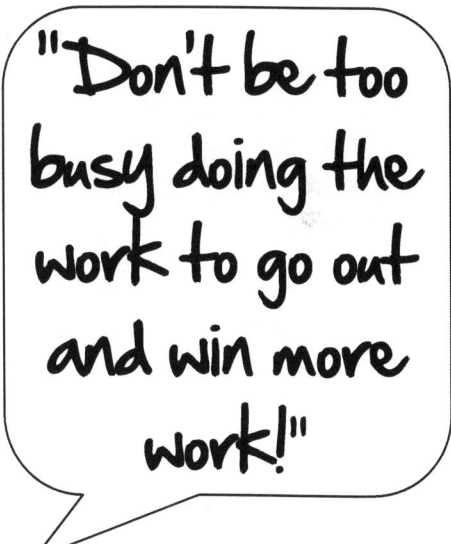

"Don't be too busy doing the work to go out and win more work!"

So, I asked her about how it worked. She said, "Well, normally, it takes me about four weeks to build a website. Then, I get paid for it. Then, I have to find another client which can take anywhere up to another four weeks." So, my thought was, why not tell the client that the website is going to take six weeks. Then spend that extra time doing some marketing so that when you've done the website you're working on now, you'll have a greater chance of having a project to move straight onto rather than having to go out there and do it?

Well, to cut a long story short, she did this. She not only sold more websites but her cash flow was far more consistent. She'd actually developed momentum and she developed a method for keeping that momentum. So, it works. Give yourself the space to develop and keep momentum in your business. When you get those first few customers, just don't stop doing the things that you did to get those first few customers in the first place. Don't be too busy doing the work to go out and win more work literally because your cash flow and your workload will be up and down like a yo-yo. It's very frustrating and it's very stressful as well.

Another thing just to add in there, and I know I've covered this somewhere else, is if you want to build momentum in your work and momentum in your business, **you have to be doing some kind of marketing or business development every single day**.

Now, that could be, if you're really busy, as little as putting out some tweets. It could be as little as writing a little bit of a blogpost. It could be developing your database. It could be sending out some emails to your customers just to remind them that you're there. Whatever it is, do it. That's the way you will keep momentum in your business.

Somebody once told me that when **you win a customer, it's just the beginning of the process**. I didn't quite get that at the time, but now I understand the logic behind it. You may have put quite a lot of effort into selling to that customer. But, once they're a customer, it's just the beginning because you still need to nurture that relationship. That was said to me quite some time ago and it never really registered at the time. If you sell

> "Getting the ball rolling is the hardest bit, so don't let it slow down!"

more than one product, it's highly likely that because they're already a customer, and if they've had a good experience with you, they will go on to buy more stuff if you prompt them to.

Use your success as a springboard

So, just be aware. Think about what Amazon does. They don't just sell you one thing. Once you're a customer, they keep marketing to you. They keep trying to draw you back and it's always based around what it is you've already bought. This is really one of the key principles of marketing and client relationship management. But, it's important that, once you get that momentum in your business, you just keep this stuff going. Even if it's just a regular push on a daily basis to just maintain that momentum, it does need to be done.

So make sure that you celebrate your successes. When you get that first customer or first few customers, make sure you celebrate. Jump up and down if that's what it takes. Say, "Well done," and shout and root and holler, whatever it is, but you need to do it. Psychologically, you need to tell your brain we're onto a good thing here because, if you don't, then winning customers just becomes blasé and you should never ever be blasé about winning customers. You should always celebrate your success.

Then, when you've got that momentum, make sure you maintain it. Getting it started is always the hardest bit, so why waste that opportunity? Keep doing the things that you were doing that got that ball rolling in the first place. If that's networking, do more networking. If it's email marketing, do more of that. If it's maintaining relationships with clients, do more of that.

A good example of this is I know a guy who's a specialist tax consultant here in Leicester who works with accountants. Now, he doesn't win work all the time every day from his clients, but he makes sure that he nurtures his relationships with them. He emails people. He phones them up, asks them how they're doing, occasionally goes out for lunch with his best clients, occasionally goes out and lunches with his clients' clients, just to nurture and maintain that relationship. He's keeping the momentum in his business going. It's a fantastic way of developing a successful business. It certainly works for him and it can certainly work for you.

So, keep that momentum going and, as I will mention over and over, make sure you're doing some marketing every day.

Your ultimate success revolves around your ability to get and keep customers.

Without that, you have no business. You'll just have a badly paying hobby.

So get out there, let the rubber hit the road, get some momentum, celebrate success, do some marketing every day and keep it going. That's how you succeed at being self-employed.

Chapter 13
Why Goal Setting Is A Powerful Tool To Help You Make Your Dreams A Reality

When you really want something you will take consistent action and make sure you get it.
"The reason most people never reach their goals is that they don't define them, or ever seriously consider them as believable or achievable. Winners can tell you where they are going. What they plan to do along the way, and who will be sharing the adventure with them." Denis Whately
What do you want? Successful goal setting depends on being very specific about what you want to achieve.

What are 3 things you would love to accomplish in the next 6 months?

If you don't know, ask yourself what are the things you don't want?

For each of the things on your list, write the antidote.

Most successful people are goal-orientated. Setting goals gives purpose, focus, direction and motivation. It is estimated that only 3% of the population has an organised goal or life plan.

"Without goals, you are likely to be drifting and, when you drift, you are not in control!"

Without goals, you are likely to be drifting and, when you drift, you are not in control. You have relinquished your basic right to shape your own future. In doing this, you also surrender your freedom of action which restricts your choices and can lead to frustration, anxiety, fear and stress.

So, are you in the habit of setting goals for yourself? Do you have a life plan? The fact that you are reading this suggests that you probably do. Congratulations!

"Crystallize your goals. Make a plan for achieving them and set yourself a deadline. Then, with supreme confidence, determination and disregard for obstacles and other people's criticisms, carry out your plan." *Paul Meyer*

This chapter was kindly contributed by Claire Gallear who is a performance coach.

Chapter 14
How to Deal with Awkward Customers

One of the things that's always overlooked in almost all of the business books that you read is awkward customers. Because no matter what business you're in, **at some point, you will get into some kind of dispute with a customer**. Something will go wrong and everybody's haunches will go up and the artillery will be loaded.

Take it from me, if you're in business long enough, this is inevitable. So, it's important to know right up front how to try and prevent it in the first place and then how to minimize the damage and repercussions when it actually happens. Notice that I'm not saying "if", I'm saying 'when' it actually happens.

Terms and Conditions

So, first things first. Before you even get started, it's very important that you have very good Terms and Conditions. Now, I can't underestimate the importance of this because I've been caught out a few times because my Terms and Conditions were weak (and at times non-existent).

However, it kind of goes against the grain of doing

> "Having well-written terms and conditions is a great starting point!"

business (and treating your customer well) by slapping down this great big document full of T's and C's.

But, the thing is, a good set of Terms and Conditions or a contract will protect both sides. It sets out the stall for what's going to happen, how the relationship is going to work and what you will (and will not) do during your relationship. And the "will not" is just as important as what you 'will' do.

It should also include things like payment terms and the consequences of breach of those payment terms. And also it can be used to limit your liability so you're not left completely open to all kinds of claims of unlimited liability.

So, it's absolutely vital that your Terms and Conditions are as well-written as you can make them right up front. There's nothing to stop you amending your Terms and Conditions as you go along, and I've had to do that on a number of occasions in reaction to situations that I've been in.

Obviously, nobody goes out of their way to upset clients, but there are times when there has been a misunderstanding and the client expected us to do something which we hadn't agreed to. Or we've done something which the client wasn't expecting, often to the benefit of the client, but if it comes as a surprise it can lead to conflict.

So, these Terms and Conditions and this agreement is, to some extent, an insurance policy. No one likes a lot of legal jargon thrown at them, but all of your clients should be made aware that these are the Terms and Conditions that you will work to.

Managing expectations

Another major problem area, especially for small businesses, is that people expect the earth. Web design is a classic example of this. Clients expect you to do loads of stuff, which wasn't originally agreed in the original discussions. It's not specific to the Terms and Conditions.

What often happens is the client will just ask you to do this little bit more, just a little bit more, and just a little bit more. This is, again, where your contract (or engagement agreement) plus your Terms and Conditions comes into its own because it's very important right at the beginning of any kind of work to know what's going to happen. And this applies particularly to services – with products it's not so challenging because it's a transactional business. If you sell jewellery online for example, you do need Terms and Conditions but, by and large, it's process driven.

> "It's important to manage clients who keep asking for more and more!"

With services, which are often customized to the client's needs, it's a little bit more difficult. You're looking at accountancy services, consultancy, business advice, website design, legal services and a whole load more.

If a product is customized to what the client wants, then it's absolutely vital to get as much as you can agreed upfront, and get it in writing (emails will do). Effectively you're telling the client: "we're going to do this to this level of standard (or to this end result). Is that what you want?" And the client will either say yes or no.

Now, here's the difficult bit. When you're working away and the client says, "Oh, can you just do this?" and it's over and above what you had originally agreed, most people – and I include myself in this - would simply say, "Yeah. No problem. It'll only take me five minutes. I'll sort it out." The problem with that - and I'm not saying you should say no - is where the client is regularly asking you to do work over and above what you'd originally agreed, suddenly you've got mission creep and it can go on forever.

I've had this situation in the past. It's not so bad now but I've had clients that would constantly be asking for bits and pieces to be changed and I ended up constantly making changes. Thus, the project never gets finished and both sides end up frustrated.

With this scenario, you run the risk of the client feeling like they're not getting what they want. but it's because you've done more and more work than you originally envisaged. I've eventually had to say: "Look. This is over and above what we originally agreed. So, I've actually given you more than we'd agreed, and more than you're paying for. We need to draw this to a close or you need to give us more money." At which point, the client can make the decision on what to do next. It sounds harsh but you're actually doing both sides a favour by drawing a line under the situation.

> "Learning to say no to mission-creep is just as important as terms and conditions!"

This has happened to me on a few occasions, and I hold my hand up and say, "Yep, it's my fault because I didn't manage it properly." So, it's important to know where you stand with your project, and with your client, and with your contract. I promise you it will save you a lot of heartache if things go awry.

So, what do you do if you do get an awkward customer?

Well, one of the first things I always do is to examine what we've done compared to what we promised to do. If we do get into a dispute, we know exactly where we stand in terms of what work we've accomplished for the client, and what results they've got as compared to what they originally wanted.

If what they've got is what they originally asked for, then we will often say something like: "We're not doing any more work on this until you examine what we agreed to do compared to what we've already done and tell us what else you think we should be doing."

This may seem like a bit of a long-winded way of doing it, and it can seem quite harsh to a client, but at the end of the day you cannot work forever on a project unless the client starts paying for extra work.

And remember: Some folks will try and take you for a ride. I hate to say it, but there are some not very nice people out there and, at some point, you will run into one or two of them. It's unavoidable.

Keeping cool!

One of the biggest keys is to keep a cool head because, if you get emotionally involved here, it's going to stress you out. Unfortunately, if it stresses you out, it's going to have a knock-on impact into all other work that you're doing. I promise it will reduce your productivity because you won't be able to focus.

> "Remember that some folks are just not very nice and will be difficult, no matter what you do!"

You won't be able to produce. You won't be able to sit down and do work on other clients because nagging you at the back of your mind will be this client who's being a real pain.

I would say try not to get too emotionally involved here. In fact, on a couple of occasions, I've handed an awkward client who's refusing to pay over to my lawyer and simply said, "Look. You better deal with this because I'm running the risk of getting very upset and, when I get upset, I'm not capable of making rational decisions."

Do you need legal advice?

Don't ever be afraid to go down the legal route if you feel that you've been fair and reasonable, but weigh it up carefully and don't get too heavily involved. **Legal action could cost you a lot more time, hassle and money**. Yes, you may have a relationship with a customer and you may have thought that they were your friend when they were being nice and friendly. But, once you get into dispute, you need to try and detach yourself from that, especially if they are being deliberately awkward. You cannot afford the mental space when you're self-employed to be dealing with just one awkward customer.

There are hundreds, thousands, maybe millions of potentially good customers out there. Why waste all your time, effort, energy, and emotion on just one miserable, awkward customer?

I know it's easier said than done. It's never going to be the easiest thing to do. But, the key is to focus on what you need to be doing now. If you get an awkward customer, do your best to put it out of mind and just deal with it.

On a couple of occasions, I've had to phone up a legal helpline because I wasn't quite sure where I stood when I got into disagreement with a client and having that kind of assurance helps. If you're in the UK you have the Federation of Small

Businesses (FSB). In my view the membership fee is well worth the money. I have come across some real stinkers of clients and having someone I could just talk to who is well qualified has been such an assurance. Trust me, it is well worth spending the money on that.

If you're not in the U.K., your local Chamber of Commerce probably has something similar whereby they offer you a legal helpline. I recommend it. Or, as you might want to do, if you've got a friend who's a lawyer, just phone her up. Have an informal chat for 15 minutes. If necessary, pay them a little bit of money. But, having somebody on tap who can give you helpful legal advice has been really useful.

> "Having somebody on tap who can give you legal dvice is incredibly useful!"

There was one project where we finished a website and the client refused to pay. It wasn't a huge amount of money. But, being able to speak to someone in the legal profession about where I stood was invaluable.

So, make sure you use your network and have somebody there who can help. There have been times when I've had to send an email to somebody and I've cc'd it to a friend at a particular law firm. She happens to be a partner in this law firm. So, that kind of puts a little bit of pressure on them if they know that a lawyer is on the fringes waiting to be involved. I'm not saying you should do that all the time but this message gets results.

Hopefully, you'll avoid it by having good Terms and Conditions and being reasonable with people. But, some people are just horrible and I'm sure you could think of a few colourful adjectives to describe them. Just remember: not everybody in business is nice. Not every customer is your friend. And you have to be able to accept that.

Make sure that whatever it is you agreed to do is in writing, emails will do.

If you're a retailer, the sale of goods is usually covered by legislation and most people are aware of their basic rights; e.g. they can return the goods if the product doesn't work properly within the regulated period.

If you sell online you're legally required to have Terms and Conditions, etc. If you provide services, make sure that the provisions relating to payment are very clear and unambiguous and agreed up-front to avoid uncertainty if there are disputes.

If you supply to some bigger businesses they will likely impose their own Terms and Conditions upon you. To be honest, I don't like doing business with large companies because they regularly abuse their position and often take months to pay. But, you can choose whether you want to work with that or not.

But if you do get into a dispute, try and keep a level head. Get some advice because you need to know where you stand.

Above all, be polite to people. If you're nice to people, you will usually attract people who are similar. I've been in business

> "And finally: move on as quickly as you can. Life's too short to stew over morons!"

in website design for five years now, and we've had just three awkward customers, and we consider that to be a fairly good ratio considering all the clients that we've had.

In all of those occasions, I've followed what I've just told you and every dispute worked out in our favour. On one awkward client we spoke with a lawyer and we decided that it wasn't worth the hassle because there's more important things to do. For the time and hassle we would spend chasing up these few hundred pounds, the chances are good we could have sold another couple of websites and it would have more than covered it. So, just move on. And that's the key here - move on. If you get into a dispute don't dwell on it, don't stew, don't get angry (if you can avoid it): just move on. **Life's too short and your business is far too important for you to be stewing over one obnoxious moron of an ex client**.

To summarize all of this, right upfront have very good Terms and Conditions - as best as you can make them - and don't be afraid to amend them as time goes on, especially if situations come up. React to those situations by adjusting your Terms and Conditions.

And make sure that you treat people fairly but don't be shy of seeking legal support where you feel it's needed.

Chapter 15
Networking - How To Make It Work For You

When you first become self-employed or run your own business, you'll start to meet other business owners and others involved in business. And at some point, you'll be invited to networking events and groups.

There's a few things I'd like to cover regarding **networking because networking can be a great way of developing your business, but it can also be a great waste of time and money**.

The first thing that is very important to networking success, and along with all your other marketing as well, is **to work out your return on investment**.

In other words, if you are in the habit of keeping a very close eye on where your customers are coming from, you should be able to tell whether networking is being a profitable investment of your time and money or not.

> "You need to know if networking provides a profitable return on investment!"

And the reason I say this is because a very good friend of mine, Garry, who used to have a playground equipment business once said to me: "You know what? I spent nearly £2,000 last year on going to networking events. But, I have no idea as to whether it provided a profitable return on investment."

Now, in business, **it's vital to know which bits of your marketing are producing a result**. This is because, if you don't understand where your business is coming from, how do you know whether any of your marketing is working effectively?

And networking is a form of marketing. It takes up time and money so you really NEED to get a decent return on your investment.

For example, if you go to a networking lunch it will maybe cost £25, ($40-ish). You might meet a handful of people and if you put those handful of business cards in a box and that's the end of it.

And you might hope that the people you met happen to be in the market for what you sell now or at some time in the near future. Or maybe they know somebody who's in the market for what you sell and that they will remember you to pass on your card or your contact details. This scenario is the networking norm and is based more on hope than any kind of marketing plan.

But I'd like to turn your networking into something a little more scientific because it can (and should) be a very powerful and profitable marketing channel.

So, first things first. Have a return on investment mindset with all of your marketing. Networking is no exception. So here's a plan to make networking less about hope and more about planning.

How to prepare to go to networking events

Your Business Cards

First of all you need a darn good business card. It's pointless having a business card which just gives your name, rank, and serial number. In other words who you are, what you do, and what your contact details are.

"Your business card needs to stand out. Try and prompt some kind of action!"

Make sure that your business card provokes some kind of action or response. Give the person holding the card some kind of impetus to visit your website, or to get in touch, or just in some way do something other than just go back to the office and shove it in a box. Your business card should drive some kind of action first and foremost.

Your 60 Second Elevator Speech

A lot of networking involves doing a 60-second speech - your "elevator pitch" as some people call it. It's your opportunity to "elevate" yourself and your business and make you stand out from the crowd. However, don't just stand up and say this is who we are, this is what we do, simply because most people would do. I can promise you that it gets nearly no response unless the person in the room likes you and is in the market to buy pretty much imminently. It just doesn't work that way. So, work on how you can make your elevator speech a little bit more engaging.

As a good example, my friend Tom, he runs an accountancy business and he stood up in a networking event one morning and said, "I'm an accountant and I guarantee that I will save you more money in tax than you pay me in fees or you don't pay at all." Now, did Tom pick up work that day? Yes, he did. Why? Because his speech was giving the audience something to react to. It was pretty much a no-lose guarantee. It was very well done, very clever on Tom's part. But, it worked because nobody else was doing it.

Most people stand up and said this is who I am, this is who I work for, this is my name of my company, and this is what my company does. No impetus for the audience to react, respond in some way. **So, your 60-second speech should be a driver of action**. It should be one of those call now kind of ads that you often see, and this is why you should call.

> "Your elevator pitch should prompt people to think and also take some action!"

Now I know that not everyone is comfortable with standing in front of a group and if you are really nervous about doing these sort of speeches, I'd suggest avoiding those events for a month or two and going to less "formal" meetings which are more of the "meet and greet" type. You don't have to spend a lot of money either because a lot of less formal events are in coffee shops where you only have to buy your own drink, or at least the cover charge is very low. Then when you do go to a meeting where you have to make a speech, you'll be a lot more confident about the whole thing.

Who do you meet?

So, the next important thing is remembering the people you meet. I would urge you to learn how to remember people's names. You will be remembered a heck of a lot more if you remember people's names because the sweetest sound in anyone's ear is their own name. And, it will always set you apart because most people don't remember and usually don't even make the effort to do so.

There are some techniques you can use and you can find them on YouTube most likely. In fact, I may even do one of my own. If you learn to remember people's names, even if it's 75% of people's names, you will be remembered because it stands out so much.

Most people say, "I've got a rubbish memory" or "My memory's really bad." Actually, no, that's not true. Your memory is just untrained. It can be trained and learning people's names is one of the best skills you could possibly have if you run a business. Simply because, when you come to meet somebody and you remember who they are and you can remember a little bit about them and the conversation that you had with them, it will stand out more than almost anything else you have to say that day. So, remember people's names. **When you do meet someone at a networking event, follow up.**

Always email people, "Great to meet you at the event yesterday. It was good chatting with you about your XXX business, or whatever it is that they do. If you think I can help in any way, please let me know. If I come across anybody who might be interested in what you do, I'll be sure to bear you in mind" or something along those lines.

In other words, you're letting them know that you're not just collecting their business cards and dumping them in a box. That's not the way to do business. It's not the way to do networking. So, follow up.

Then, when you've followed up, make sure that you **add all of these email addresses and names into some kind of email marketing, or CRM system**.

and keep in touch.
When I meet someone at a networking event, I put their business card, give it to an admin assistant, she puts that information into my CRM system, and I keep in touch. People go on our email list and we send them out useful stuff. So, never be afraid to keep in touch.

The thing is, if you meet someone at a networking event, it could be the only time you see them. But, it could well be that three months later what you have to offer is what this particular person needs. And if she or he doesn't remember you, if you haven't followed up, if you haven't kept in touch, there's no way you're going to be in the running to supply what that person needs.

> "Always, always, ALWAYS follow-up when you meet with people at networking events!"

So, let's be logical here. Ideally, **follow up within 24 hours of meeting the person**, and then add them to your email list, and keep in touch. Adding people to your database is an absolute key to success in networking and, to be honest, success in marketing too.

Networking events are also a great way of picking up referrals - not just for you, but for others. When you're at a networking event, if somebody says, "Oh, I could do with such and such," make a note on their business card and follow up even if it isn't what it is you do because, if you email them the following day and say, "Look, I heard you were interested in finding a new accountant. Here's the name and number of my accountant. He does fantastic work and it won't cost you anything to talk to him. Go and give him a call."
Now, *that does a number of things in the mind of the person you've been speaking with.* First and foremost, it lets them

know you were paying attention, which to be honest in these very busy times, attention spans are shorter than ever and people remembering things is rarer than ever. So, again, you can stand out. It also lets them know that you think about them, not just in terms of another potential customer, but as somebody you can help.

The more you go out to help people, the more successful you will be in networking.

As a good example, I recently met a woman at a networking event. She'd not long started a management training company. When I spoke with her about what we do, which is web design, she said, "Well, I'm having my website built at the moment." I said, "Oh, that's okay. Not a problem. Is there any other way I can help you?" She said, "Well, I want to do more networking." I said, "I'll tell you what. Give me your card. I'll send you an email with a handful of networking events which I think will be useful to you, and you can get in touch with the organizers and go along."

And that's what I did. She followed up the following day and I sent her a list of a few networking events that she could go to. I added her to my email list and, funnily enough just over a month later, she came back to me and said, "Do you think we could talk about you building my website?"

Now, if I'd just taken her business card and said, "Oh, well, that's nice. Good luck with your website," that could have been the end of it. But, because I followed a process of making notes, offering to help, following up, keeping in touch, then a few weeks later she became a lead for some work. Was it worth the effort? Of course it was. The networking event was free. It didn't cost me anything there. It cost me a few minutes to write an email. My admin helper sorted out putting her details into a database. And she phoned me a few weeks later.

Have a follow-up process

But, the point is, I have a process for doing this and so should you. It doesn't matter where you are, where you start, always have a process. Working out what people say at the event, remembering their name, making notes if required and keeping your promises are very important things to to when networking.

> "Having a proper follow-up process will be a huge help with developing leads and sales!"

If you say you're going to do something do it. In business today, you will only be as good as your word. In other words, if you say, "We can deliver this service and product by then," you've got to do it. If you say, "I will follow up by then," you must do it. If you say you're going to send someone an email, you must do it. If you say you're going to phone someone back, you must do it. There are no exceptions to this rule.

Hopefully, networking won't be so terrifying to you. If you do have to get up and do a 60-second speech, and you've never done that before, please practice. But, bear in mind that everybody starts somewhere. And, even if you're so nervous you can barely speak, a lot of people in the room are going to be sympathetic.

I really want you to succeed in networking because for a lot of very small businesses and the self-employed, it's a fantastic marketing channel.

Chapter 16
Why It Takes More Than Just Passion To Be Successful

Over the last few years we've heard loads of talk about 'passion' and how you need to get across your passion for your product of service. Folks saying things like 'Follow your passion' or 'passion is the key to success'.

I've heard people at networking events say something like: "I'm passionate about helping people".

I even heard a client of mine say "if I get in front of potential customers they'll see my passion for what I do and want to buy".

Well I'm going to say the same to you as I did to my client: "That's absolute bullshit!"

Now, I'm not suggesting that you shouldn't have any passion for what you're about and how much you care about what you're up to. Heck, I'm passionate about helping self-employed people get more out of their web presence and business marketing. But very rarely, in my experience, does anyone buy something from someone because of their passion.

> "Turn your passion into something that will help your clients, then they will buy!"

People only ever buy something when they've been convinced that there is something in it for them if they part with some money.

Don't believe me?

Think about this: when was the last time YOU bought something because the person selling it was passionate about it? Go on, surprise me.

OK, I know this goes against some things that many folks seem to believe and apologies if you're passionate about your business, product or service. But I think it's vital that you're clued up early-on about what will make the selling difference in your business.

I know we all have a passion for something. Some folks are passionate about their football team, some about music or musicians, others about politics or religion. And there's nothing wrong with any of that (OK, so maybe the football...).

What I'm saying is that your passion is an inward thing and will have limited impact on your ability to bring in customers and build a business.

What will make the big difference in your business is when you turn that passion into clear benefits for your potential customers. And that is the job of your marketing approach (which is discussed in Chapter 9).

Don't get me wrong here, I do believe that you should be passionate about your business. Without that passion you'll quickly lose interest. But please, do yourself a favour and focus on client benefits. Turn your passion into something that will help your client.

Chapter 17
How to Coach Yourself Out of Mental Blocks

Have you ever felt there's something blocking your motivation but you're not sure what it is?

I've experienced this.

You can discover the truth in lots of different ways. You can just be told it, you can read it. If you start looking at things from different perspectives, you realise the truth. It's very powerful when you do this for yourself.

Some things have held people back for years, they're very strong. They've probably heard the truth from other people possible hundreds of times but they haven't accepted it.

If you ask yourself enough questions, eventually, the truth's going to emerge.

Let me give an example from my own life. When I started coaching I had a mental block about selling coaching - which is a bit of a hindrance if you're trying to start a business.

I decided to coach myself by filming myself on my camera phone. I didn't know what I

"Mental blocks can hold you back, sometimes for years. So the sooner you get them dealt with, the better off you'll be!"

was going to say, I was just speaking from my heart. I just expressed what was going on in there. I got it all off my chest. I talked about the subject, about selling. How I felt about selling and other people selling to me.

And what came out was that I don't like manipulation. This is a bit of a hot button for me. I have been manipulated, as a lot of people have, in their lives. I became aware that the thought of it generated almost an anger in me!

What had been holding me back was this aversion to manipulation. I'd been subconsciously associating it in my mind with selling. I'd thought "I can't do that! I can't manipulate people!".

As I watched it back, I saw myself thinking "I'll have to manipulate if I'm selling"

I answered "Actually, do you?"

"Hang on a minute! No you don't!"

Once I realised that this was my mental block I was able to switch it round.

The opposite of that, for me, is a passion for giving people freedom of choice.

I asked myself: *"Could* I offer my services in ways that honour my passionate values of freedom of choice and respect?"

And of course when I asked myself that question I came out with all sorts of answers.

"If I make myself available, people can approach me! If I'm sending emails or publishing articles people can read it when they want to."

"If people know about me, if I explain what I do clearly enough, then people have freedom of choice to avail themselves of my services or not."

Now I was feeling captivated, focussed, energised, relieved and happy! I had opened a door of creativity.

But the point that I'm trying to get across is: I wasn't aware that the subconscious thought was holding me back, until I started exploring it, until I started talking out loud.

I mean it's probably obvious to you, but to me it was a breakthrough!

When I see other people set free from their mental blocks, sometimes that they've had for years, I find it deeply moving.

For me, that's my purpose for being here. I feel kind of inadequate and a bit hypercritical about it because, although I have been set free in a lot of areas, I still need more.

What's your mental block?

Try filming yourself talking about the topic, and then watch it back. Interpret your reactions on your face and your body language.

You may be believing something that's not entirely true.

This chapter was kindly contributed by Claire Gallear who is a Performance Coach.

Chapter 18
How to Deal with Staffers

If you're running a small business or you're self-employed, the chances are good that almost everyone you know has a job, and it's also likely that they've never been self-employed or run a business themselves.

I like to call these people 'staffers'.

Now, one of the biggest challenges with these staffers is that they will never fully understand what it's like to be self-employed and, as a result, are usually unable to offer proper support and advice for you when you need it.

You see, when you work for somebody else, you can usually get away with just turning up to work, coasting for a bit, and making yourself look busy (as long as you don't do it too much). Most folks who work for someone else can also leave their work at the office and rarely have to bring stuff home.

"Very few staffers will understand the challenges of self-employment!"

If you're self-employed, the picture will be very different to that; you're likely to constantly be living your work simply because you're it. Coasting or just looking busy means that you don't get paid.

The thing you need to be aware of is that many of these

people will try to give you advice, but it's based on their own working experience. Unfortunately most staffers don't realize the issues that you have with organizing yourself, with going out and winning the work, with going out and delivering the work, with managing the accounting, with organizing your day, and all the different constraints and challenges that most people have when they're self-employed.

When you go to work for someone else, typically your work is provided for you, your work place is provided for you, and usually somebody else is doing all the motivating. So, it's difficult for them to understand what it's like to be self-motivated at times.

When you are self-employed, you have to be it. You have to find your own motivation. No one is going to fire you. No one's going to threaten to take you to discipline if you're not performing. If you don't perform, you don't get paid. It's that simple.

So, what should you do if you need help?

Well, one of the things I like to do is to surround myself with people who are also self-employed.

And I'd pick on a few good people you get along well with and ask them if they'd be willing every now and then just to meet with you to kick some stuff around, share some problems, help one another out. And, funnily enough, you'll find that people are often willing to do this because they understand the challenges and there's an awful lot you can do to help one another out.

Asking a staffer to do this, now even if this staffer is a partner, or your wife, husband, or whatever, can be a very great challenge because they don't understand what it's like to be in the shoes of someone who is self-employed.

So, find someone who's in your boat. Chances are good you know a few people in your networking circles who can help you out. There's loads of places you can go. It could be that you create your own mastermind group where you troubleshoot one another's problems, share issues, encourage, and inspire one another to do well and to get stuff done.

> "Find someone who is also self-employed and ask to help each other out!"

The key is to be honest. Now, when staffers try to give you advice, I'm not saying that it's all going to be bad, there might be some nuggets you can take out of it, but be aware that they will never understand where you're coming from with your challenges.

Having said that, there are some amazing benefits that go with being self-employed.

A couple of years ago, I took an afternoon off to go and watch my oldest daughter take part in her school sports day. And, interestingly enough, there was only me and two other parents there -- only three parents there watching their children doing sports day and we were all self-employed. And, when I told some friends of mine who were staffers, and they said, "Well, that's okay for you. You can do that because you're self-employed." But, what they didn't see was that I was awake until late that night catching up on the work that I'd missed. Being self-employed does give you that flexibility, but the staffers just don't see that extra effort that goes into it.

And then there's money -- I hate telling staffers how much I charge. My charge out rate can be as much as £150 an hour for some of the specialist work that I do. When they hear that, they instantly assume that I'm making megabucks. But what they don't see is that I'm not charging £150 an hour for every hour of every day. There's an awful lot of work that goes around that in terms of marketing, and administration, business development, feeding back to clients, etc. And they don't understand that. They just see the top line figure, "£150 an hour! He must be loaded!" And it just isn't the case. And it's difficult to get it across to them sometimes.

> "Telling staffers your hourly charge-out rate can be a dangerous thing!"

Staffers will rarely understand that there are times when you just don't earn anything, sometimes for days/weeks on end. Whereas, staffers can go to work, spend a few hours making it look like they're working and, as long as they don't do it too much, they'll still get paid. When you're self-employed that doesn't apply and if you don't work, you don't get paid. You don't have a salary.

So, here's a thought on how to deal with staffers who don't get your work. One of the things I try and do is simply say, "Yep. You could be right. But, that's not how it works." And, then, I try and explain to them what's it like and some of the challenges. Some get it, some don't, it doesn't matter.

The key is this: You're going to get advice from people no matter what they do. Staffers, unless they've been self-employed, are going to struggle to understand your challenges. So, surround yourself with people who can help to balance it out a bit.

Chapter 19
How Getting Proper Rest Can Actually Help You And Your Business

I want to encourage you to stop and take a rest, a real rest, regularly.

Do you always feel like you haven't done enough? But when is enough?
When you're absolutely exhausted?

You see, we need to stop looking at our businesses and look at ourselves for 5 minutes!

So let's stop slave-driving ourselves and acknowledge all the things we've successfully accomplished in the last month!

We'll always have opportunities to set ourselves new goals. But everyone needs rest!

But, did you know, **rest actually stimulates creativity**?

Research published by Psychologists Ap Dijksterhuis and Teun Meurs of the university of Amsterdam* discovered unusual

"Getting proper rest will actually help you to be more creative and get a lot more done!"

and fascinating ideas about creativity and the unconscious mind which are simple to understand.

Imagine two men in a room. One of them is highly creative, but very shy. The other is clever, not as creative and far more domineering. If you were to ask them to come up with ideas to advertise a new product, true to form, the loud but not especially creative man dominates the conversation. He does not allow his quieter counterpart to contribute, and the ideas produced are good but not very innovative.

Now imagine a slightly different scenario. You again ask them to come up with advertising ideas but distract the loud man by getting him to watch a film. Under these circumstances, the quiet man is able to make his voice heard. You walk away with different, far more creative ideas.

The quiet guy represents your unconscious mind, it is capable of wonderful ideas, but is often difficult to hear. The loud guy represents your conscious mind – clever, not as innovative, but difficult to get out of your head.

This means what you will probably find as you wind down and consciously switch off from thinking about your business, is that you will experience innovative ideas popping into your head.

When that happens, don't jump up and run to your office and start working on the idea! Just record the key points in some form or another so you can think about them after your break.

So, try these practical steps:
- Acknowledge your successes in the last month
- Give yourself regular rest, daily, weekly and monthly
- As you rest during your breaks, have a notebook handy and jot down ideas that come to you.

You don't have to spend huge amounts of time on this but

one of the hallmarks of very successful people is that they give themselves regular time to rest, switch off, relax and reflect.

* A. Dijksterhuis and T. Meurs (2006). 'Where Creativity Resides: The Generative Power of Unconscious Thought'. *Consciousness and Cognition*, 15, pages 135-46.

This chapter was kindly contributed by Claire Gallear who is a performance coach.

Chapter 20
Why Increasing Your Fees is a Good Idea

In this chapter, I'm going to talk about money and, more importantly, the money that you charge customers for what you do. You see, when you run a small business, most people misunderstand pricing and value in the mind of the customer.

Now, we're not going to get into a debate on price versus value in this session. I've written a chapter on Setting Prices. But, for right now, I just want to talk about pricing and I'm going to give you a couple of examples of where increasing your prices can have a very beneficial affect on your business and why putting your prices up is a good idea.

The low price model
So, let's start with a quick example. A few years ago when I started our website design business, I thought that being cheap and value driven (or price driven) was the way forward. And it was great because I picked up quite a few customers quite quickly. But, I realized that I was actually making very little money at all. I was working fairly long hours and actually producing very little profit. The low-price model wasn't working.

> "Upping your prices can have a very beneficial affect on your business!"

So, I had a chat with a friend of mine who is a business coach and she suggested that I double my fees. Now, I have to admit that doubling my fees was a terrifying prospect because my instant reaction, just like most people's reaction, was that I'm going to lose all my clients. And her response was this, **"If you double your fees and lose half your clients, what have you really lost?** Certainly not money."

So, I had to think about this and, despite my initial fears, I did double my fees. Funnily enough, it didn't reduce the number of clients I had at all. All of a sudden, my income doubled. But, what it did was eliminate a lot of clients that I probably shouldn't have had in the first place.

Those were the clients who were already worried about the price. They didn't want value, they just wanted all the work done for the cheapest possible price. What I found was that if they whinge about the price they will whinge about so much more.

It's ironic, isn't it, that those who want the best deal are often going to be the most awkward customers because they're in the mindset of driving a hard bargain. And to be honest, you have to ask yourself, do you really want those clients?

So, in doubling my prices, I effectively priced myself out of this particular band of customers. So, now, I sell my websites for more money than I've ever done and I get better clients than I've ever had.

Now, I'm not saying that doubling your price in your market is going to be a good tactic because you may well

> "Doubling your fees may not work in your business but there will still be scope!"

price yourself out of the market completely if you do put your prices up by 100%. It depends on your business and whether your market are price-driven or value-driven- you need to do your research before increasing your prices to see how much you can charge.

But, here's another example. A very good friend of mine, Tim, he's a plumber and he's very good at what he does. He's a lovely guy, very good with his customers. He's personable and he gets a lot of repeat business. But, Tim's problem is that he's way too busy, constantly busy.

Checking the numbers

Don't get me wrong, good plumbers usually are very busy. So, I suggested to him a number of times that he needs to put his fees up by a little bit. And his instant reaction was just like mine: "but I'll lose a load of customers". And my response was, "Yeah, Tim, but if you increase your prices by just 10% and lose 10% of your customers, what have you lost? Your income stays about the same, but it means you've got 10% more time to focus on other things, like developing repeat business or learning something else that can be sold where that expertise and knowledge can be sold at a higher price."

So, let's have a quick check through the numbers here. And I'm going to run through some very simple maths. So let's imagine you have a business which sells soap. It doesn't matter what product but let's just stick with soap because everybody uses soap (well, most people do). Imagine you have 100 customers who spend £100 a year with you. So, your turnover is £10,000 a year. Now, imagine that you put your prices up by just 10%. So, if all your customers stayed with you, you would all of a sudden be earning £11,000 for that year. Everybody would be happy with that, instant pay rise of 10%. Most people who work in the civil service would be overjoyed at a 10% pay raise. But, bear with me.

Long-Term Success

And now you think, "Okay, Karl. That's great. But, I'm going to lose some of my customers." And, yes, you probably will. But, just for arguments' sake, let's say you lose 10% of your customers. All of a sudden, you've got 90 customers paying 110 pounds each a year. So, you've lost 10% of your customers, but you've increased your prices by 10%. Now, that gives you 9,900 pounds for the year. And you think, "Well, actually Karl, my income has gone down by 100 pounds." But, here's the good news: You've got fewer customers, which means you're going to be spending less time serving customers. You've increased your prices by 10%, so all new customers pay that higher price, but your income has gone down by just 1% and you bought back 10% of your time.

And the chances are good that all of those people who are no longer customers are people who are only there for the price anyway. They probably don't appreciate the value of what you have to offer.

You could do this with all kinds of different things. But, as I've mentioned earlier, **when I doubled my fees, it had no impact whatsoever on my business. I didn't lose any customers. As a matter of fact, I get better customers now than I've ever done**.

And I know for certain that, if Tim increased his prices by just 10% even to his newest customers and not the existing ones, the chances are good no one would complain because, to be honest, if your bath is leaking, or your shower doesn't work, or your central heating has blown up, it's not always about the price, it's about getting it sorted out quickly.

So, the point I'm trying to make here is this: **Increasing your prices can be very good for you!** Now, if you're in a business which is incredibly price sensitive that may not necessarily work for you. But, for the most part, most businesses, especially smaller businesses, could do with more income and the most effective way of doing that is to increase your prices.

The only place in my experience where price is a problem is in between the ears of the business owner. Let me reiterate that. The only place where price is a problem is between your ears. Think about it. If price was an issue, Mercedes Benz and all of the luxury car dealers would have gone out of business a long time ago. All the luxury goods we have, such as Rolex watches, wouldn't be sold anywhere. Nobody would buy them if price was the problem. It's not about the price. It's always about the value.

> "Remember: it's not usually about the price, it's almost always about the value"

So, my challenge to you is have a think about whether you can up your price by just 10% as a starting point and see what happens because, to be honest, 10 pence on the pound, 10 cents on the dollar, isn't a huge amount of money. Rarely will people miss it. So, don't worry about the price, worry about your business and its profitability.

Oh, and at the time of writing, Tim had put his prices up by 10%. Did he lose any customers? No, not one. The real difference is that he's now able to afford (in both time and money terms) to take his young family on holiday to France for a couple of weeks.

Chapter 21
What To Do When Things Get Tough!

In this chapter, we're going to come onto a very difficult area and that's what happens when things go wrong.

Ultimately something will go wrong in every business. **Very rarely is self-employment a smooth exercise.** You will have challenges. You will have stresses. You will have awkward customers. You'll probably have difficult suppliers. At some point, something will happen which is not good.

"Don't be deluded – things will go wrong at some point!"

One of my big frustrations about a lot of the personal development books is that they don't tackle this. They tell you to go out there, and be motivated, think positive, but they don't actually tell you what to do when it hits the fan. And I promise you, if you've been in business long enough, it certainly will hit the fan.

And when it does hit the fan it will cause you stress. It's likely to cause you to have some sleepless nights. It's also possible that there will be times when you really don't want to get out of bed because you don't want to face it.

So, now that I've painted such a gloomy picture here's my

thoughts on tackling all of this because you have to face up to this stuff.

You see, being self-employed is not an easy option. In fact, being self-employed in many ways is far more difficult than having a job. You often work longer hours often for less money than you would have had if you had a job. You have to deal with a wide variety of issues in terms of your clients, product and service fulfilment, accounting and bookkeeping, marketing. In effect you're dealing with everything that would be dealt with by dedicated departments in big businesses. And it all revolves around you.

So, what do we do when things do go badly wrong? Well, one of the first things I find is very important is to **talk it over with somebody who is also self-employed**, but has been in the game a little longer than me.

This may seem a bit like counselling and, to some extent, it is. But, one of the absolute keys when you're self-employed is to make sure that you have friends who you can go to.

I'm not saying you go around their place for a whole day and take up all of their time. It could just be as simple as a 20-minute phone call saying, "Look, I'm having this particular issue and I'm really struggling. Has this ever happened to you and how did you tackle it?"

> "Find someone who's been there and done it who can offer a helpful word or two"

The key thing, and it may seem daft, is that even if they don't give you an answer that's particularly applicable to you, just getting it out of your system to a sympathetic ear will have a massive benefit.

Psychologically, it means that you actually offloaded it, to some extent, onto somebody else. And in doing so your mind will feel more at ease and is likely to start working on problem-solving.

Obviously, you need to say it in confidence but, psychologically, you need to get this out of your system. If you simply bottle it up, it will make a mess of you from the inside out. It will harm you because it will have an impact on so many other areas in your work and your ability to function in your business will be grossly impaired. So, first things first, get it out of your system.

The next thing I would urge you to do is to **build a routine**. One of the things that people with depression are often counselled to do is to make sure that they have some kind of routine in their life. I'm not saying that being in business is going to give you depression, but the same psychological rule can be applied to someone who is self-employed and is having a hard time. You can use that to your advantage. So, make sure that you have a routine.

> "Having a routine will help you to stay on track!"

That could be as simple as getting out of bed, getting the kids to school, getting to the office (or to the kitchen table if that's where you work) and then setting out a timetable for your day. It could be something like: Between 9 and 10 I'm going to do some marketing. Between 10 and midday, I'm going to work on this client. I'm going to have a half hour lunch at midday. Back to work at 12:30 and I'm going to work on this particular item. And so on.

Put it in your diary to impose some kind of routine because the last thing you want to be doing, when you're not feeling brilliant, is wondering about what to do next. Otherwise, your brain will start to mull over all of the negative things that you could possibly think of, even things that you hadn't even considered right now. Your brain just works that way. Whatever is in your head in the minute will attract more things in keeping with your mindset. So, it's important to give yourself that routine. Literally, write it in your diary, "This is what I'm doing."

One of the things that I always do and it has worked incredibly well, is I live by the mantra, "**The day's not until the next day's planned.**" So, the idea behind it is that you're never hitting your desk wondering what to do in the morning. It should never happen. You should always have a list of things you want to get done.

Don't stop doing the things that you would ordinarily do in your business just because something is winding you up. **It's important to have this routine and stick to it.**

It's also important, at this time, to remind yourself why you're in the game. Things are going to be tough from time to time. There will be times when you don't have enough money or enough customers. There will be occasions when you have too much work. And, funnily enough, as sometimes happens in small businesses, you have loads of work and not enough money in the bank. Cash flow is a bizarre animal, but we will cover that in the chapter on finance and managing money.

> "The day's not over until the next day's planned!"

Long-Term Success

The key is to, again, remind yourself as to why you're in the business.

If you're the breadwinner for the family then the motivation is actually very strong indeed. But, you need to have in your mind the picture of why you're in the game. Occasionally we all wonder why the heck we're doing it. I still do it, despite the fact that I love what I do and I'm moderately successful at it. But, it still comes with its challenges.

Five years down the road in our web design business we still have ups and downs. There are occasional times when I don't want to get out of bed because things are just so overwhelming. But, I also know the triggers to keep me going and, from a personal perspective, it's my family. I want to provide for my family. I'm not the sole breadwinner in the family, but my contribution is important. I want us to have holidays. I want us to be able to afford school trips.

There was a time in our lives when we couldn't even do that. So, think about the reasons why and then tie that into your routine. When you come to your desk or come to your workplace in the morning, you know exactly what you need to be working on and 'why' you're doing it.

> "The routine and knowing your purpose keeps you going!"

What will often happen when you're struggling is that you will do work or what is perceived as work, but you'll end up just tinkering. You'll go onto Facebook (or any other social media) to do a bit of 'marketing' and end up reading a load of rubbish that your friends and family have posted. It just wastes time.

When you're having a hard time, you need to try to sort things out and get back to a more positive stage of mind; the feeling that things are going well. So, keep the marketing up. Keep aiming at winning customers. When you win a customer; celebrate because it's a good thing. There's millions of people out there, billions, who don't have that ability to celebrate success like you can.

But, above all, it's your routine and knowing your purpose that keeps you going when things get tough. Things do become difficult and don't ever let any of the motivational speakers tell you that it's not going to be anything other than challenging at times. It's just delusional to think that you're never going to have problems.

If you're fairly new to being self-employed, this may be a bit of news to you. But, it's better that you know this stuff sooner rather than later. So, make sure that you have all of the above things in place. **Make sure you've got someone you can talk with.** Develop a relationship with somebody who is also self-employed. That's where belonging to certain business groups can come into its own. I have a handful of people I can pick up the phone to at any one point and say, "I'm really having a problem with this. What would be your take on the situation?" I know that I'm going to get an honest opinion. I don't want somebody to sugar-coat things. If I'm being an idiot, I want them to tell me that they think I'm being an idiot. If I'm making a mountain out of a mole hill, I want them to tell me such. You need to have that honesty.

Then, if they do help you and their advice helps you to work things out, just make sure you give something back to that person. You can either take them out for dinner, buy them a decent bottle of wine, or something else. Make sure that you say or do something tangible to say thank you.
Hopefully, what I've discussed in this Chapter will arm you sufficiently to tackle the tough times. This is what I've done

and it worked incredibly well. I learned all of this from other business owners, so it has obviously worked for others as well.

So, get someone to talk to. Get a routine. Celebrate whatever success you can. And, ma-ke sure you've internalised your reason for doing what you're doing.

> "Give something back to those who help you!"

Chapter 22
Realising That You Are It!

When you start your own business, one of the most important things to realize is that you are 100% responsible for your success or failure. I'm not saying that you need to blame yourself if thing go wrong. There's a variety of reasons why businesses don't succeed and many of them are down to lack of knowledge and experience. And, to some extent, that's nobody's fault initially.

But, that doesn't mean you have to stay that way.

The point I'm trying to make here is that, when you start your own business, you always have good intentions. We all do. But, those good intentions are sometimes dented when things don't go the way we would like them to. And many people start their businesses from a position of lack of knowledge, or even worse, naivety.

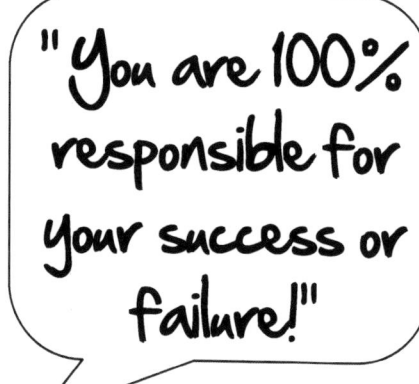

"You are 100% responsible for your success or failure!"

In my view, far too many people just think that putting out a handful of emails is going to instantly bring a rush of customers to your door. Or that putting out some social media means that you can get thousands of followers and the phone's going to start ringing. It doesn't work that way.

So, the key with taking personal responsibility is to realize that, if there's something that isn't going well in your business, you have the opportunity to examine and improve whatever it is that's not going well. And the thing is, it's a case of constantly learning. Nobody is born an expert in business. Nobody who starts a business for the first time is instantly a successful businessman. We all have a learning curve.

One of the biggest travesties I see in businesses are people who start their own business but just refuse to learn. They've learned a particular technique or they've been sold a particular methodology of doing things, and when they try it, and they try it again, and they try it again, and they try it again and it simply doesn't work.

So, my point in this piece is just simply to say: **"You need to take responsibility"**. If something isn't working, you need to take responsibility to try and fix it. Make the right decisions and get some learning.

If you don't know enough about marketing, there's plenty of marketing help out there in the world.

If you don't know enough about selling skills, there's plenty of opportunity to go and learn more selling skills. There's thousands of free videos on YouTube, thousands of articles you can download that will help you improve your selling skills (or almost any skills).

If you don't know anything about finance or managing the money, again, there's no excuse for not knowing how to do this stuff. The tax man isn't going to be sympathetic if you owe him a load of tax

"There's no excuse for not learning more about how to make your business a success!"

and you simply say, "I didn't understand how bookkeeping works". You have to take responsibility.

If something isn't working, improve it. Take some courses, buy some help, get some coaching. But don't sit there complaining, just work hard to improve it. If there are people in your business who aren't working particularly well and you don't know what to do about it, get help.

The point I'm making is that YOU have to take ultimate responsibility for these things.

You can't blame the economy because many businesses survive and even thrive when the economy is in decline. You can't blame negative people around you because you don't have to hang around with negative people. You can't blame your background because there are plenty of people who came from really challenging backgrounds and ended up being very successful.

Lack of education is not even an excuse any more. There's so much knowledge available to you on the internet for free. Even if you're suffering from a lack of confidence, there's lots of stuff you can do to improve your confidence, but you need to take responsibility.

Ultimately, when you get the hang of taking responsibility and realizing that "you are it" in your business, then things will start to change. What will begin to happen is that you will develop the habit of looking for solutions to problems. Business is a constant exercise in problem-solving, so along the way you'll learn how to be resourceful and tenacious.

The one thing I would urge you to do is to *appreciate that just because things aren't going well now that they have to stay that way*. We all like to take credit when things are going well but it doesn't always go well. Whatever happens, good, bad, or indifferent, you are responsible. I'm not saying you should blame yourself for it going wrong. But just ask yourself these kinds of questions: What can I do today to make things better? What can we do to improve on what we're doing? It isn't working, what can we do to make it work?

There's one other thing that I do need to say, and that you might have heard the phrase, "Winners never quit and quitters never win." But, I want to turn that slightly on its head because, if you're working a plan which is just never going to work in the marketplace, no matter how persistent you are, you're never going to get great success.

> *"Things will happen. So you need to learn how to be resourceful and tenacious!"*

It's a bit like selling VHS tapes these days. You could be the most passionate person about VHS. You could have the best stock of VHS videos. You could have the best VHS marketing. You could be determined to make it a success. But, you're selling the wrong product at the wrong time to the wrong market. I hate to say it but you're NEVER going to sell many more than just a few VHS videos. Things have moved on.

I know that this chapter probably flies in the face of what we're told by many of the self-improvement and motivational 'gooroos' but ultimately it's vital that you learn to take personal responsibility for what's going on.

I know plenty of people who've failed in business but did so because they didn't take responsibility for results. **Many were naive in thinking that just having a business based on a single good idea or product is a guaranteed route to**

success. I know for certain that many of them simply didn't do enough (or even any) marketing, some didn't manage the cash-flow well enough, and others didn't understand, or even try to learn, how to sell. The key with these things is that all of those things can be learned.

Up until 2008 I had a training business and in the Autumn of that year the phone stopped ringing. Even my regular clients, many of whom were big companies, just fell off the radar. When I started making calls to find out what was going on they all told me that they weren't allowed to spend money on anything other than essential things. The bosses at the top had decided that the recession meant that belts had to be tightened. The upshot of this was that I was out of business almost overnight and at the end of 2008 I was forced into bankruptcy.

But did I blame the government, the bankers, (although they both managed to avoid taking responsibility for their part in the global financial meltdown) or the economy? No. I simply had to conclude that my business model wasn't sustainable in a recession. My services were only a viable proposition when business confidence was good. Unfortunately for me, training is often one of the first things cut when business gets tough. I could easily have pointed the finger but it would have been a pointless exercise. I could have let going broke ruin me and make me bitter but it would only have been a toxic way to go.

Now I look back and realise that my marketing wasn't good enough, my database wasn't targeted enough and

> *"What are you doing today to make things better?"*

my website was not nearly good enough. And these are all things that I could have improved upon if I'd been observant enough. Like many people at that time, it just never occurred to me that the good times would end.

It wasn't an easy time and I ended up working in a couple of jobs that I didn't enjoy simply to pay the bills. But the key thing is this: I didn't blame anyone else. I took responsibility, learned the lessons and moved on with more determination not to make the same mistakes.

These days my marketing is more consistent, my website gets great results and our database is much more finely tuned. These things now mean that our results are more consistent, despite the economy.

At this point you might be tempted to say something like: "Yeah but my circumstances are different!" And my answer to you would be: "Maybe, but **what are you doing today to make things better?"**

So, look at what you're doing and always be looking for ways to improve. If there are areas where you're not doing so well then look for help, go out and learn what you need to make your business better and more successful. Never let yourself down through lack of knowledge.

But, remember, **the buck stops with you in your business. Circumstances happen to us all but it's what you do about it that makes all the difference. YOU ARE IT!**

Chapter 23
Improving Your Business With CRM And Automation

In this particular section, I'd like to cover something which has become increasingly important in the business world in recent years, and that is all about Contact (or customer) Relationship Management (CRM) and automation.

Now, as your business starts to flow, I would recommend that, as early as you possibly can, you start to automate and systematise as much as you possibly can. This will make your life so much easier than if you do it all manually.

The benefits of a good CRM system

This is where a decent CRM system can really come into its own. CRM is effectively just a database, but it's a database that triggers off activities and events depending on other activities and events. That could just be dates, certain emails, visits to your website, filling in forms, or tracking sales and reminders of activities, etc. There's an awful lot of stuff that you can automate to help with your customer service, your sales acquisition, your lead generation, and lead follow-ups.

> "A good CRM will save you countless hours by automating a lot of repetitive, low level manual tasks!"

So, I'm going to explain the main principles of using a CRM. Of course, you'll have to do your own research on how to make it work for your business according to your type of business and your type of client. **But I cannot understate the value in a CRM.** We did a lot of this stuff manually for years and, now we're beginning to automate a heck of a lot and I promise you, it makes your life so much easier. Yes it costs money but, once you've invested the time in getting it setup, the hours that it can save you later is immense. And, like I said, I cannot underestimate the value that this will bring, especially the perceived value of your business in the mind of your clients and potential clients as well.

So I've written a list of things you could automate. I'm not going to cover anything in too much detail because there simply isn't space. But this list is just a starting point, the possibilities for automation are almost endless. You'll have to discover how to get the best results for your own business as your business develops and you identify how you want to use the system.

Website Enquiries
You can set up your CRM system to do auto response to web inquiries. You can then automate an ongoing dialogue with your potential customer or the inquiry through the CRM system. You can use it for capturing lead data through your website as well. Again, you set up an automated process of social media engagement or email engagement with your client.

Follow-Ups
But it can also prompt you then to follow up. You set the CRM system to prompt you to phone them or to get in touch with them to follow things up from there.

Event Registrations and Follow-Ups
You can also use a decent CRM system to do event registrations and follow-ups as well. If you've got your CRM

system hooked up to your social media, you can also use your CRM system to do quite a bit on Twitter, Facebook and other platforms.

Networking Contacts
You could also use it to automate connections with networking contacts. You can put them into your database and have the system email out some useful stuff that's personalized to them and, also, you can gain social media followers and improve the automation process.

> "Automated sales follow-ups is a quick and easy way to improve sales success!"

Automate Social Media
I would strongly recommend using a system such as Hootsuite (hootsuite.com) to manage your social media from a single point. You can schedule social media engagement, tweets, and posts. Again, it just saves an awful lot of time and hassle by not having to login to each of your social media individually each day.

Sales and Lead Management
One thing that CRM is particularly good at is automating callback systems, which is particularly useful if you have a complex and prolonged sales process. You can use it to assign leads and inquiries to certain people in your sales team or certain elements of your sales team and to make sure that follow up actually happens.

Now, I can't underestimate how much a CRM system can help you with your sales pipeline. In our website design business, our sales process isn't lengthy, but it's certainly a sales **process**. Using a CRM system to track how many leads come in versus how many turn into appointments, versus how many then turn into proposals, how many of those proposals then turn into clients and, ultimately, the amount of money that those clients bring into the business can help you to work out your inquiry to sales ratios.

For example, suppose every ten leads turns into three customers and your average sale is £500. If your target sales for that month is £3,000, you'll need 6 customers. That means that you need to find 20 leads to generate that income. It can be very good for focusing your mind on lead generation and the numbers you need to hit your turnover target.

"You can use a CRM to monitor and improve sales conversion rates!"

But, again, you can't do this if you don't have some way of tracking those leads and tracking those conversion ratios. A CRM system can help you do this. Also, it can help you focus on the hottest leads too, based on the number of interactions with those potential customers. So sales funnelling is always a very important element to a decent CRM system.

Engage With Potential Customers
One other thing that a CRM can also help you do is to stay engaged with people who haven't yet bought from you so that they won't fall by the wayside. It will enable you to keep in touch. Even if they don't buy from you, it's worth keeping in touch because they may ask you to work for them at a later date, or recommend you to someone else. The value of keeping in touch is huge.

A number of times we've pitched for a website and haven't

won it, but because we kept in touch, a couple of years later, the client came back for a rebuild or they got upset with their web designer and they came to us. So, if you don't stay in touch, if you don't keep your company name, your branding, your marketing messages in front of them, then you're going to lose those potential opportunities. They do happen and a CRM can certainly help you to do that.

Personalising Your Messages
CRMs can also help by personalising your message, even if it's just using the contact's first name on a personalised email. Don't be afraid to personalise your messages. Even bulk emails can be personalized.

Welcome and Induction Process
The CRM system is also a good way of keeping new customers by encouraging them to feel like they're part of something by automating the welcome and induction process, especially if you need to send out resources to clients and prompt them to start accessing helpful information or training modules. You can also schedule regular emails that go out to clients to help them in some way.

Encouraging Repeat Business
Now, more specific to e-commerce and retail businesses, one of the things that are particularly good about a CRM system is it can remind customers to buy again based on timelines. So, if you worked out that every three months or so most of your clients will buy something, you could actually send out recurring prompts for people to get back in touch and to buy every three

> "Encouraging repeat buying is made much easier with automated marketing!"

months. If it's automated, it means you don't have to think about it and it happens automatically.

If you do have an e-commerce site, and use an e-commerce platform such as Magento, then you can also use email re-marketing systems (such as www.swifterm.com) to send out automated marketing emails based on your customers buying behaviour.

Recovering Abandoned e-commerce Shopping Carts

You could also use a CRM system to remind customers about abandoned carts. You could use it to create a popup system; whereby, if somebody looks like they're going to leave an abandoned cart, it gives them an opportunity to stay and buy something at a special offer or a special price. For example, you could offer them a discount if they buy within the next 24 hours. Again, it's a great way of salvaging sales using a CRM system.

Recover Customers with Expired Credit Cards

You could also use CRM to stay on top of soon-to-expire credit cards. This is one of the biggest frustrations for businesses that have online subscriptions and online memberships. What often happens is that memberships expire when the related credit cards expires, which means you lose a client.

Many people don't renew unless they've been given a reason or a prompt to renew when their credit card expires. You just lose a customer and, usually, you don't even know it's happened. So a CRM system can help you to make sure that you've got the latest payment information from your customers.

Track Email Engagement

You can track email engagement and you can tell whether people open your email. You can look at reports from your CRM system on your email marketing campaigns to see who's opening them. What a good CRM can do is, if somebody clicks on certain links in your email to look at certain information, you can program your CRM to respond to what they clicked on with further information or further questions.

It can seem a little bit Big Brother-ish, but the point of it is that you're automating the follow-up system based on the behaviour of people in your marketing funnel and your marketing channels. It can be a brilliant way to maximize the potential for a contact to become a lead and then to become a client.

Not only that, but open rates on your email marketing can have an effect on deliverability. A lot of ISPs monitor open rates of bulk emails very closely. If you have a very low open rate on your emails, a high delete rate or a very low response rate, some ISPs will even be reluctant to give your emails priority when delivering them and some may even block your emails altogether. This is because these factors could be an indication that it thinks that your emails are SPAM. So your CRM system can help you monitor this by tracking open rates and response rate.

Client and Customer Surveys
One thing that we have started doing more of is customer satisfaction surveys. It can help you to work out ideas for improvement in your business.

Asking for Referrals
You can automate the asking for referrals, or send-a-friend schemes, or whatever you have in your business. If the CRM

Long-Term Success

system takes care of it and you'll be developing your business without even thinking about it. It's happening for you. It's a great automation tool.

Improving Customer Relationsips
Another good way to use your CRM system is to include clients' birthdays so that the system can remind you to send them a birthday card, even if it's just an e-card. This is particularly good for long standing clients who you want to look after. Now, everyone in the business world get Christmas cards from clients and suppliers, but very few people think to find out the birthday of a client and to send them a card. Your CRM system can certainly help with that.

Monitoring Stats and Conversion Rates
There's an awful lot more routine tasks that you can use a CRM system for. As I said before, monitoring stats and conversion rates is a biggie. It's always good to know how many people you've got coming in as leads and how many of those leads convert into customers.

> "Automation is essential if you want to develop long-term success!"

Choose Your System
So I hope that's given you loads to think about with respect to a CRM and automating system. We use a system called InTouch (intouchcrm.com). We find it to be very good and we've even fed back to them to help them develop it. There are bigger systems, like Infusionsoft (infusionsoft.com), which can be quite expensive, especially if you're self-employed you get an awful lot for your money. Other systems like Zoho (zoho.com)

do an awful lot as well for a manageable fee.

There's a lot you can do, but I would say, if you want to develop long-term success, long-term profitability of your business, you really need to automate as much as you possibly can. A CRM system is one of the best ways of doing that. Ultimately, the right CRM should more than pay for itself in terms of how much extra business it can help you bring you but also in the amount of time it can save you in not having to constantly do repetitive, low-skill, low-level tasks. So research the best CRM system for your business and automate as much as you possibly can.

Chapter 24
Moving From Self-Employed to Business Owner

This is a very important chapter if you've been self-employed for a while because, at some point, you're likely to be faced with the decision to move from being just self-employed to being a business owner.

Now, let me make a distinction here. When you're self-employed, usually it's just you. You are it. You're the business. You're responsible for doing everything. That includes sales, marketing, administration, invoicing, finance, product delivery, everything. You're it. But, as your business progresses, the chances are good that you're going to find that there's only so many hours in the day and that you struggle to get stuff done. That's quite common so don't panic, there are things that we can do.

This is the point where you need to start thinking a little bit more about moving from a self-employed mentality towards a business owner's mentality. So I'm going to cover that in this particular chapter because there are important considerations for doing this. And I'm going to use my business as an example of where I went from self-employed, working from home, to

> "You're moving from a self-employed mentality towards a business owner's mentality!"

having a business and having people working for me with greater profitability and also much greater freedom and flexibility with what I'm doing.

So here's how the story goes. When I started the business I was working from my kitchen table. Nothing wrong with that. Most self-employed people start there, or they work from a spare room in the house. It was okay for a while, but I realised that I wasn't as productive as I knew I should be because I felt that there are far too many distractions at home.

Getting Out Of The House

So I asked a friend who rented an office if she had a spare desk I could rent from her, and she said yes. So I paid her a fee every month, and I started going to the office every single day. It was also near to my daughter's school, which meant I could do the school run (a real bonus).

It was costing me a little bit, but I quickly realised that my productivity went up, which means that my profitability went up as well. I was more organized, more focused because I was at work, and there weren't the distractions at the office that I had at home.

Now, fast forward 17 months, and my friend Erica decided to give up the office so I thought I'd take over the lease. Again, worth the investment because of my increased productivity. And what's even better is I rent a couple of desks to other self-employed people to help pay for the office.

Being Taken More Seriously

But what I found in the mind of my target market is that, **as soon as you get a business address, people begin to take you that little bit more seriously**. They think you're a proper business because you work from an office.

I don't know why (in this world of freelancers) that working from home is still seen as quite a lowly thing to do. But having an office and having a business address made a big difference. It enabled me to increase my fees as well because, suddenly, there was a perception that I'm actually a business rather than just somebody working from a kitchen table. I don't know why this is so, I may never know, but I don't care.

"As soon as you possibly can, get someone else to do your bookkeeping!"

Getting a Bookkeeper

So beyond that, then I also realised that there were a lot of things I needed to get rid of in terms of what was happening in my working day because they were just taking up too much time and causing me too much stress.

The first one I did was bookkeeping. I would urge you, as soon as you possibly can, get someone else to do your bookkeeping. It's a pain in the rear job. Very few people really, really look forward to it, but it's important to have it done. There are bookkeepers out there who are more than cost-effective. My bookkeeper, I think, costs me about 18 pounds an hour, and she's worth it because I hate bookkeeping. It's just a drag, and I often put it off. So my books for a while were in a bit of a state because I never got it done. Now, it gets done, and it's out of my hands. It's no longer a headache. It just gets done by somebody else.

Offloading Admin Stuff

The next step was, also, then to begin to find people to do other stuff in my business. Fiverr.com (fiverr.com) is a great resource for this kind of stuff. So I'd get people to do various bits of administration and transcription as well. This book is being written, having been recorded on an audio system. The audio files get transcribed by a wonderful woman, Janet, from a company called Zoom Transcription, and it means that I don't have to sit there at a computer writing away because I'm not a particularly fast writer. I enjoy it, but it just takes me a long time. I can record roughly 1,000 words in about seven minutes. To type 1,000 words would take me at least two hours. To me, that's a fantastic time-saver. Someone else can do the legwork, and I can get on with doing other stuff such as developing my business.

Higher Level Technical Help

On top of that, then I realised that to grow my business I'm going to need to get some help. I was on the lookout for somebody to help me with design and project management. As it happens, a very good friend of mine, who was particularly good at that, said, "Great. Why don't we work together? I'll pay you for the work that you do, and if I can help you and some of your clients, it'll work well." So we set up what was originally a subcontract agreement. Now, we're more like business partners on a lot of projects.

> "What else can somebody else do that will free you up to focus on more important stuff?"

But the point is that I could get a lot more stuff done, and I can sell more because I have somebody else handling what, in my view, is quite a time-consuming part of the product delivery. So it means that this part gets done by somebody else, and I can go on and do more strategic stuff.

On top of that, I felt the need to get somebody to do a little bit more of the programming and website development. I found somebody who now works for me part-time, who's a great programmer, lives not far away, and comes into the office a few times a month. It just means that, again, I can contract out more of this stuff so I can focus on more strategic business issues.

Becoming a Business Owner

What's interesting, and I know it's a risk, is that doing this stuff was the most logical next step in my business in that, if you want to grow a business, you have to realise that you cannot do it all yourself. There just are not enough hours in the day. So you have to get help.

Doing this stuff has enabled me to develop a business, and now I do very little of the design and website building myself. I'm able to focus on business and project management, and also marketing and product development. And having all of these things going on around me has enabled me to write this book. It's enabled me to develop other products and services. It's enabled me to go on and do other things to boost the profitability and

> "If you want to grow a business, you have to realise that you cannot do it all yourself!"

marketability of the business. And I would have struggled if it was still just me.

It Doesn't Have to Be Just People Doing Stuff For You

What about using more technical resources to help? For example, we deliver training with our websites, and a lot of clients were asking me for additional help or to be reminded of what to do because they didn't update their website on a regular basis. So we're developing a training website whereby they can log in and take a look at a load of videos on how to do common stuff. It means that they're less likely to phone me, which cuts down on unnecessary interruptions. I can point them to the resource, and they can use it over and over again.

It's a system, which enables me to not have to spend time doing the same things over and over again. It's delivered remotely. So are there ways that you can do this too?

If you read the chapter on automation and CRM you'll discover loads of ways to use technology to do some of the work for you.

Focus On Your Role In The Business

But the point of it all is this: Ultimately, in your business, you should only be doing the stuff that only you can do, and that will be the mission-critical, strategic-management business development stuff. I urge you, as soon as possible, to look for ways to get other people to help you with certain things. Bookkeeping is an easy one. But, is there product delivery stuff that you can get done by somebody else? In our business, we get blog posts written by other people. Can you contract out some of that so it saves you, again, the hassle of doing it so you can focus on your business rather than constantly be working in it?

The point of this chapter is this: You should only be working on the things that only you can do. If you want to grow a successful business and be successfully self-employed, you have to acknowledge that there aren't enough hours in the day to get everything done. There never will be. There's never nothing to do. If you want to grow a business, you've got to get help. There aren't many people who, all on their own and working from their kitchen table, make big bucks. It may not be what you're doing it for but, if you want to grow a business, you can't do it on your own.

> "In your business, you should only be doing the stuff that only you can do!"

So look for ways to get help. Look for ways to farm stuff out. There are loads of other self-employed people running their own small businesses that would love to help out. There are bookkeepers, admin support, product delivery people, blog writers, you name it. That's just the beginning. The sooner you get to grips with this, the easier your life will be, and the more successful you will be longer term. It will enable you to create not just a successful business, but a sustainable, long-term business as well.

The Next Step

The next most-logical step in business is to go through the process of actually employing someone properly. This will mean setting up a payroll and having all of the compliance boxes ticked (insurance, policies etc).

Many consider this to be the riskiest part of growing a

business. Having staff gives huge benefit but it's not a topic we have space to cover in this book.

The thing to remember is: nobody will share your enthusiasm for your business. So hire slowly and fire quickly Take your time to find the right person but get rid of them quickly if it's not working.

Resources

If you like what's in this book and want to learn more then I have a page of resources on the Smashing Self-Employment website.

Just visit : www.smashingselfemployment.com/book-resources

The page includes templates and additional help with some of the topics covered.

Additional Reading

The Game Changers by Paul Chapman and Julia Roberts

Eat That Frog by Brian Tracy

The 4 Hour Work Week by Tim Ferris

The One Thing by Gary Keller

Build Your Business in 90 Minutes a Day by Nigel Botterill

Made in the USA
Columbia, SC
02 April 2018